EVERYDAY LEADERSHIP

YOU WILL MAKE A DIFFERENCE

BRIAN UNELL

Clovercroft Publishing

Published by Clovercroft Publishing, Franklin, Tennessee

Edited by Justin Spizman, Angie Kiesling, OnFire Books, Adept Content Solutions, and Hilary Unell

Cover design by Brian Unell and Debbie Manning Sheppard

Interior design by Adept Content Solutions

Printed in the United States of America

978-1-954437-66-1

CONTENTS

INTRODUCTION

EXPANDING LEADERSHIP

Growth springs from better recipes,
not just from more cooking.
—Paul Romer

There are tens of thousands of books on leadership. Chances are, you've read a few yourself. As this is being written, there are more than 57,000 books on leadership on Amazon, and this desire for leadership lessons doesn't seem to be waning anytime soon.

There are fables such as *The Five Dysfunctions of a Team, Who Moved My Cheese?* and *Our Iceberg Is Melting* that share the impact of change. There are books on creating an organizational purpose like *Start With Why* and self-help leadership books like *The 7 Habits of Highly Effective People* and *Good to Great.* There are books by well-known and highly successful people (at least as measured by wealth) like Oprah, Arthur Blank, Jack Welch, Robert Iger, Ray Dalio, and some guys named Michael—Dell, Bloomberg, and Jordan—who all share their "secrets to success" and their learning experiences along the way.

I've read many of them, and all have something to offer. Great leaders have a "growth mindset" and as a result lean on other leaders for their ideas, insights, and learning experiences. And while all the people mentioned above are supposed to be wonderful people, they probably won't take your call or meet you for a cup of coffee, so reading about their leadership philosophies is one great way to understand what made them successful. As I navigated my own journey as a leader throughout the years, I've come to realize how different so many of us are, and how valuable this ongoing learning (and communication) can be. There is no one way to lead. No matter how prolific any icon or author is, there's no one-size-fits-all formula for leadership, because what feels right for you may not be right for someone else and what worked perfectly yesterday may not work tomorrow, as every situation is different. Each one of us must find the path that fits best when it comes to leading individuals, organizations, families, and teams. This expedition of leadership development is the process of expanding yourself and your ideals as a leader.

In the pages to follow, I intend to share things that I've been through in my personal and professional life, so you might glean something for yourself. Leadership is as random and impactful as it is hard to explain. Yet as random as it may seem, great leaders are easy to identify—as are the not-so-great ones. In the end, you can learn what to do and, more importantly, what not to do from the best and worst respectively, because we are all a product of the leaders around us.

Whether intentional or unintentional, chosen or merely given to us, I do know that leadership really matters, whether we realize it or not. The effect of leaders in someone's life is illustrated by the saying: "You are the sum of the five people you spend the most time with." I'll expand this even further to say that just one great leader can have a phenomenal impact on someone's life, as well as on an entire organization or family for decades and generations respectively.

My dream of writing a book started about eight years into my career after I attended a keynote address by Patrick Lencioni. His pragmatic approach, which focused on vulnerability, transparency, and trust, resonated. His energy was infectious, and he exuded passion for

---

This expedition of leadership development is the process of expanding yourself and your ideals as a leader.

---

leadership. And the idea of making a living by helping people and making organizations better seemed like the ultimate job—because for me it would not be a job at all. Cultivating talent and helping others become successful have always given me the greatest sense of personal and professional satisfaction. But I have always been analytically minded and grammar challenged. In fact, I grew up hating reading (at least all the "classics" for school), but after I finished Patrick Lencioni's *The Five Dysfunctions of a Team*, I realized I actually really enjoyed reading. I had just hated what I was reading up to that point.

My favorite leadership books are the ones where the author provides a nugget about or a slightly different view into something I have seen time and time again. Like Matthew Kelly's *Off Balance*, where I learned about the concept of "professional satisfaction," or Liz Wiseman's *Multipliers*, which describes my own leadership style better than I can describe it myself, or *It Doesn't Have to Be Crazy at Work*, which outlines many unconventional ways the authors run their company, Basecamp.

While you would never apply everything you read, these "aha" moments in leadership ignite me to think differently and can help the leaders of tomorrow build their own creative best practices.

And that is what this book attempts to do.

In the following pages, I am going to:

- Share tangible, real, authentic stories about Everyday Leadership.
- Demystify leadership by taking the concept of leadership off the pedestal and bringing it to the ground level so that everyone can access and apply the underlying concepts of Everyday Leadership.
- Challenge the notion that leadership is exclusive; in fact, Everyday Leadership is actually inclusive.
- Expand leadership from businesspeople to teachers, coaches, parents, clergy, government officials, frontline supervisors, and everyday heroes like firefighters, police officers, nurses. More importantly,

I want to expand it to the next generation so they too can have the opportunity to practice Everyday Leadership.

- Show that leadership is neither a singular path nor a linear progression towards a destination. Instead it is a practice and a journey of minor adjustments (I like to call them tweaks) and improvements you make along the way.
- Give you freedom to read this book in one of three ways:

  1. Pick a vignette or section of vignettes that you want to explore, learn from, and focus on to improve your Everyday Leadership.
  2. Read it cover to cover to gain insights and perspectives on how others may see Everyday Leadership.
  3. Never read it at all, kindly doing your part in donating to my children's college fund and supporting their opportunities for Everyday Leadership.

My hope is that you do read this book, share it with others, and (most of all) find something for yourself within. Whether it be transforming your opinion of leadership, giving you a fresh outlook on strategies you can use in life and business, or helping you to realize that we are all leaders in some fashion, my goal is to expand your overall perception of leadership beyond boardrooms, clubhouses, and locker rooms so you bring it into your life each and every day.

I am doing this not because I want to simply change your mind. Rather, I want to help you realize that we all have the opportunity to equip and empower others, inspiring them to take positive action to change how they live and relate to others at home, at work, and in their community. A lofty goal? Perhaps. But just one impactful and intentional leader can offer others the opportunities to learn and grow that will make today better for you and me, and tomorrow better for the generations that follow.

I want to help you realize that we all have the opportunity to equip and empower others.

In summary, leadership is everywhere. It's inside of you, and inside of me.

Everyone can and should strive to demonstrate leadership every day, wherever they are. And that is what makes this book so special—it celebrates and encourages the unknown leaders, the little leaders (like our kids), and those who maybe wouldn't be considered leaders in the first place if we applied the traditional definition of leadership.

Everyday Leadership is a decision, and whether you turn the page, both figuratively and literally, is up to you.

PERSPECTIVES WHEREFROM GRANDPARENT TEAM
UNDERSTAND BUSINESS EXECUTIVE LOCKER ROOM
TOGETHER HELP OTHERS HOBBIES EMPOWERING
SOLVE MORE PROBLEMS THAN YOU CAUSE IMPROVE
COMMUNICATION CANDID THINK DIFFERENTLY
TOWARDS THE FUTURE BELIEVE POSITIVE INTENT
INCREASE YOUR KNOWLEDGE BEST SELF-AWARE
INTEGRITY CLARITY
RELATIONSHIPS GROWTH MINDSET GENUINE HUMBLE
SEPARATE FACT EXPECTATIONS
TEACHER FAILURE IS NECESSARY CONNECT THE DOTS

CHAPTER 1

WHAT IS EVERYDAY LEADERSHIP?

Definitions belong to the definers, not the defined.
—Toni Morrison

What's your leadership philosophy or style?
It's taken me many years of observation, curiosity, and trial and error to develop my own "brand," which I refer to as Everyday Leadership.

Throughout my career, I've encountered many different types of leaders. Some were strong, some demanding, some more reserved, some believed management is the same as leadership (which it is not), and others who just didn't seem to know how to lead people effectively. I took what I learned and observed from each one of them, as well as other sources (books, articles, research, TED talks, etc.), and defined my own brand of Everyday Leadership that's practiced daily but focused on the long term. It can be best described as empowering, collaborative, and hands-on. It is based on mutual respect and being relatable, available, and approachable, while focused on learning, growth, and understanding. I don't just sit in an ivory tower and tell people what to do; I provide a framework of my expectations (which are high), define and live my ways of working (which are clear), value and recognize the contributions of every team member (which is necessary), and provide them opportunities to expand their knowledge, skills, and experiences (which is empowering).

And when you can do this effectively, I've found you can achieve amazing results. For example, I have delivered hundreds of millions of dollars in revenue improvements, created shared service centers that consolidated hundreds of resources to deliver services more effectively and efficiently to internal and external customers, developed a business case for a $180 million technology system replacement and was co-leader of its implementation, and built and led teams of more than 1,500 people. While all of those are tremendous accomplishments, I am most proud of creating a culture where leaders were empowered, and frontline team members had the knowledge, tools, and resources to do their jobs. This led to an environment where turnover was reduced by more than 50% and employee engagement scores improved dramatically.

Because I truly believe in the approach outlined above, it is easy for me to live it every day through my communication and my mindset—the focus of this book.

My philosophy is to foster an environment that allows individuals and teams the opportunity to achieve their maximum potential. When you create these opportunities for the team to grow, rather than just handing out orders or telling them what to do, it gives people a choice and an opportunity. It also gives them the freedom to think, challenge the status quo, improve, discover new solutions, and reap the rewards and benefits that allow them to become their best selves by gaining experience and building confidence while delivering results.

Over time, I have realized that I derive significant personal and professional satisfaction from cultivating talent, and at the midpoint of my career, I decided it was time to make a career transition. I had a great job with a wonderful organization, but to continue to grow my

---

My philosophy is to foster an environment that allows individuals and teams the opportunity to achieve their maximum potential.

---

career I needed to "leave my comfortable seat on a very good airplane" and jump out. Some would call it a mid-life crisis, but (at least in my mind) it was a thoughtful, contemplative, and deliberate midlife decision.

Upon learning of my departure, hundreds of people across the organization reached out with their wishes for continued success. Among the emails, cards, phone calls, and personal encounters, I was truly humbled by the several dozen people who recounted a story about something I did or shared something I said that had a profound impact on them over the years.

As the stories were being shared, there were a few I clearly remembered, a few more that sounded vaguely familiar, but for the vast majority I did not remember them at all. This got me thinking: How I could make such a memorable impression on someone (actually dozens of people) but not remember it personally? Was it because my memory is terrible? Quite possibly, but as I reflected, I realized it was because the vast majority of the interactions were not planned and just happened during the course of a normal day of being human.

To help me figure out what would come next, I started working with an executive coach. The first thing she recommended is that I spend time trying to understand and define my "brand." As a result, I asked a dozen or so people to answer the question: "What is Brian's brand?"

While I received feedback from many of my experienced leaders, the most impactful response came in the form of a letter from an executive assistant just starting a career, who wrote:

"BU ... Be You

Not sure how to make this a branding statement or if this is even what you meant but if I had to sum you up, this would be how:

Although you have this esteemed title that most people automatically think would come with a corresponding attitude of (maybe a little warranted) arrogance, you're so grounded. We come from different backgrounds, career levels, beliefs, eras, etc. but somehow you managed to be this relatable easy to talk (to), present professional person that has characteristics that I aspire to have when I reach the heights of my professional and personal success. I am so grateful that I was able to join the organization under your leadership because it has given me a perspective on leadership that embraces authenticity respectability and efficiency. I know now that you can be a leader who is straightforward and kind, realistic and creative, responsible and relatable, resourceful and valuable, objective and respectable, professional and personal and orderly and messy and I just value that so much…. The next organization or business you create will be so lucky to have you. I don't know what anyone could possibly tell you to change but I would say to continue to be you, BU. ☺️"

While very few people have the initials BU, in order to be an effective leader you need to "be you." In the quest to expand our skills, wisdom, and wealth of knowledge regarding leadership strategies, and to impart what we learn to others, one thing is certain: leadership must be authentic.

And for me, being authentic means doing my best to practice Everyday Leadership. Since Everyday Leadership is designed to expand leadership, I don't think it should be defined but instead described:

- It is a practice and a journey not a title, role, or destination.

- It continuously focuses on improving those around you.
- It requires intentionally and constantly learning to enhance your own tools, concepts, skills, knowledge, experience, and abilities.
- It is the art and science of leveraging, applying, and executing three elements:
  - **Traits:** Knowing who you are/what defines you
  - **Growth Mindset:** Leveraging what you know and your propensity to continually learn (tools, concepts, skills, knowledge, experience, abilities)
  - **Culture of Empowerment:** Creating an environment where those around you can make themselves, the team, and the outcomes better

Everyday Leadership is one's ability to recall and filter through these items and apply the right one at the right time while demonstrating behaviors that others value. This singular trait is the true differentiator of people who others respect enough to value their opinion, follow them, and execute to get desired results.

The A to Z of Everyday Leadership:

As we unpack Everyday Leadership, you will find that this special concept is a bevy of many different factors. Of the ingredients listed it can sometimes be all of these, just a few of these, or even none of these. My point is you, as much as anyone else, define Everyday Leadership. To that end, let's unpack this concept in even more detail:

- **A**ssumes as little as possible but also has a strong intuition.
- **B**elieves there are no boundaries but knows where others' lines are.
- **C**onnects on both an intellectual and emotional level.
- **D**emonstrates curiosity and a growth mindset.
- **E**nsures communications are purposeful and expectations are aligned.
- **F**eels empathy for others.
- **G**oes beyond just checking a box to connecting the dots.
- **H**onors those who built the foundation for them to be successful.
- **I**nspires others to live these values.
- **J**uggles multiple inputs/priorities.
- **K**nows when and how to step in and engage (managing vs. leading).
- **L**ives by the same moral compass, no matter the situation.
- **M**anages others up instead of keeping them down.
- **N**eutralizes negativity.
- **O**perates with character, integrity, and consistency, especially in times of uncertainty.
- **P**romotes vulnerability over invincibility.
- **Q**uestions ideas, not people.

- **R**ecognizes the views and perspectives of others.
- **S**eparates the BIG from the little and helps those around them do the same.
- **T**ells the truth; Yes! All the time.
- **U**tilizes tools, knowledge, and experiences appropriately.
- **V**iews others' actions with positive intent (until they show otherwise).
- **W**akes up every morning thinking about what they could do better.
- **X**-rays the situation to see beyond the surface.
- **Y**earns to improve the outcomes of others.
- **Z**ooms in and separates facts from fairy tales.

CHAPTER 2

YOU CAN MAKE A DIFFERENCE

*I alone cannot change the world, but I can cast a
stone across the waters to create many ripples.*
—Mother Teresa

When I was growing up in the 1980s, leaders were
tough, strong, invincible. "Greed was good."
Organizations were structured to be top down. While
earning my MBA and master's in health administration
in the late 1990s, philosophies and practices began to
change. But change can be slow, and not all industries
move at the same pace. As a result, there was a conflict in
my learning. The health care industry was still operating
as if it was the time of the Industrial Revolution; it used
traditional command-and-control leadership models in
which employees were incentivized by money and told
what to do. However, my MBA classes introduced other
concepts, such as creating cultures focused on purpose
while empowering, trusting, and recognizing the team.
This conflict continued through my consulting career

as my Big 5 employers were moving towards the newer empowerment model while my clients, where I spent the majority of my time each day, were in health care. The newer concepts of leadership were reintroduced to me by Patrick Lencioni in 2007. He opened my eyes to a world of possibilities, but it took a longer time and a lot more help to go from grappling with those concepts to the book you are reading today.

To be an effective leader over any significant duration, you must be vulnerable, relatable, and credible.

Although it may not become apparent until you finish the book, this chapter in many ways is a summary of all the concepts of Everyday Leadership. It provides context to the words on the front cover and shares the journey we go through, the challenges we face, the choices we make (or don't make), how solutions can be right in front of us but at the same time invisible, the importance of recognition, the need to share (and hopefully realize) our dreams, the risk of putting ourselves out there for others to critique, and the impact we can have on others and that others can have on us. In addition to reading the words on the page, I encourage you to count the number of people, moments, and decisions that all together provided the necessary support, guidance, coaching, and encouragement to generate the words you are reading...

For approximately a decade, I had been keeping ideas and thoughts in the notes section of my iPhone in hopes of one day writing a book. For most of that time, my wife was the only other person who knew of this idea, and I was quite sure I would never do it. For years, I would constantly ask myself, "Who am I to write a book?" I would follow this question with lots of other thoughts and facts, demonstrating why I am neither qualified nor talented enough to write such a book, heck any book for that matter. Then you add onto it the time required to do this, sprinkle in my risk-averse personality and penchant not to stray too far from my comfort zone, consider my complete lack of knowledge about what it takes to write a book, and round things off with the belief that I'm a terrible writer. To be frank, all this

---

To be an effective leader over any significant duration, you must be vulnerable, relatable, and credible.

---

led me to be a nonstarter on my path to becoming the next Tony Robbins, Simon Sinek, or Patrick Lencioni. But my thumbs kept typing ideas into my phone, so I typed. And typed. And typed. Note after note, using so much of the valuable space on my iPhone just to compile and deposit ideas week after week, month after month, and year after year, even when I thought there was very little chance I would actually do anything with them. So outside of the occasional comments to my wife, I kept the concept of writing a book to myself—too scared to share and too worried about how others would judge me in today's world, where everyone can be a critic, using Tweets to pick things apart and tear people down.

But over the years and through a series of conversations, my desire only grew. I eventually felt inspired enough to take the risk to write this book. It started with a comment from a colleague, Jyoti Rajagopal, who is one of the smartest people I ever worked with. She told me one day that my thoughts and ideas were "insightful." A small comment but one from someone I respect tremendously and trusted as a colleague made me think that perhaps I did have something valuable to offer/share with others.

A half-dozen years later, as part of leadership development course, I made a split-second decision by volunteering to share a "dilemma," where I explained my idea and desire to write a book. This was followed with the reasons why I shouldn't do it. The exercise was structured so that after my brief introduction of the dilemma, the other twenty or so attendees who were health care administrators and physicians got to ask me questions and then discuss and debate the dilemma as if I was not in the room. I had known and worked with many of these colleagues for years, learning about leadership concepts and our own leadership characteristics/tendencies, as well as developing relationships and building trust. However, it still felt like a huge risk to make the split-second decision to share this dilemma. If I shared this "secret" and put this remote dream in the public for others to critique and confirm my fears, doubts and insecurities, it seemed it could ultimately crush my dream (even though I thought the chance of realizing the dream was remote). To my pleasant surprise, the feedback (both during the formal session and since then) was extremely positive. My biggest takeaway was "other than time, what do you have to lose?"

As a couple of years went by, I continued to compile more and more thoughts, and I shared my dream to write a book with more and more people. Then, in 2017 I took a friend and colleague named Shay Eskew to an Atlanta Braves game. Shay is a world-class Ironman triathlete. That, in and of itself, is an accomplishment, but as a child, Shay was burned on over 65% of his body, endured dozens of surgeries and years of rehabilitation, and lives with the scars every day. When you know this, you quickly realize that Shay is more than an athlete. Shay is an inspiration and one of the most positive people I've ever met.

Knowing Shay's story, I told him that he should write a book. He looked at me and said, "I am." And he started to educate me on the process and cost, confirming all my concerns. Nevertheless, I shared with him that I too had always wanted to write a book. In November 2018, Shay completed and published his book *What the Fire Ignited: How Life's Worst Helped Me Achieve My Best*.

Ever since I shared my desire to write a book, Shay had regularly checked in to see how my book was coming along... knowing full well I had not even started it. But his inspiration and confidence in my ideas and me has gone a long way to help me go on this journey.

Then in December 2017, I was invited to meet with some colleagues from Accenture, one of whom was a woman named Kristin Ficery. Kristin is an extremely accomplished leader and has a unique ability to connect with others. Somehow during our discussion, I mentioned that I was thinking of writing a book and she said, "You need to speak with my friend Molly." If you've gotten this far, you know that when I say, "try new things," I must mean it! I did a lot of due diligence in my desire to try this new thing, and I wasn't going to leave any stone unturned.

A couple of sentences later I learned that "Molly" had successfully pivoted her career, including writing a book on leadership. And it turns out that "Molly" was actually Molly Fletcher. As a huge sports fan, I knew of Molly Fletcher and her story. For those of you who may not know, CNN once described her as the "female Jerry Maguire." As one of the first female sports agents, Molly recruited and represented hundreds of sport's biggest names, including Hall of Fame pitcher John Smoltz, PGA Tour golfer Matt Kuchar, broadcaster Erin Andrews, and basketball championship coaches Tom Izzo and Doc Rivers. Molly successfully negotiated over $500 million in contracts and built lasting relationships, she also observed and adopted the traits of those at the top of their game.[1]

Molly was gracious enough to give me thirty minutes of her time. Molly is no nonsense and straight to the point. She asked me to describe my high-level thoughts about my book. I explained I wanted to share vignettes

---

1   https://mollyfletcher.com/about/

of my experiences and observations from which others could learn. She asked me to share a couple of the vignettes that would be the basis for the book. So I shared that communicating well and setting clear expectations are critical to success (see chapter 4) and the important distinction between being right and being correct (see chapter 8). Molly's response was "Those aren't bad." And she followed up by saying something like "typically people think they have content but don't; you actually have some good concepts to work from."

And my response was, "Thank you, but I'm a terrible writer." Molly responded immediately, "That's not a problem, I know a great ghostwriter here in Atlanta." And with that sentence I learned there are others out there who I could get more help from. So I asked for the name of the ghostwriter, and she replied "Justin Spizman." And I responded with significant doubt, "the attorney?" Molly said "I think he may be an attorney, but he is the guy who helped me write my book. He's awesome and I can introduce you." I thanked her and said, "I think I know him."

Five years earlier, looking for some variety in my exercise routine, I started playing pick-up basketball and met a guy (who happened to be one of the better players) named Justin Spizman.

After speaking with Molly, I searched the internet for Justin Spizman. And sure enough, it was the same person I thought it was. In February of 2018, I formally reached out to Justin for the first time. For all the reasons shared, plus the fact I was working (more than) full-time with an infant and almost 10-year-old in tow, I just could not commit the time and energy to the book then. But Justin and I stayed in touch. Although he probably would have bet money I never was going to follow through, the stars aligned in early 2020 for this project.

But my story doesn't end there! And that's where the unexpected events came in. Once we had a solid manuscript fleshed out, I wanted to get feedback from some trusted colleagues before publishing it. So I asked a handful of friends to preview the content, and one of my former bosses (Norma Zeringue, who is now an executive coach herself) was gracious enough to do just that. Norma offered constructive feedback. I shared that I thought writing was going to be the hard part, and as challenging as it was, I explained that the marketing and publishing part of this journey has been much more difficult for me. In fact, I felt like I had been dropped into the middle of a jungle with very few tools to find my way out. Norma offered to connect me with someone who had gone down this road before—Bethany Williams. She was gracious enough to give me thirty minutes and told me about OnFire, an editing and publishing think tank that helps authors and speakers. I looked them up and after some vetting, I engaged them to look at the project to see what I might be missing. They edited and reviewed it for ways we could strengthen the connection with the reader and connected me with Clovercroft Publishing.

The point is it's easy to become negative about your dreams and your capabilities but with the right attitude (see chapter 10), deciding to overcome my weaknesses (see chapter 13), getting out of my comfort zone (see chapter 14), demonstrating curiosity (see chapter 16), and asking lots and lots of questions to gain insights and help from others (see chapter 17), I was able to turn the dream into reality. To quote Tony Robbins, "The only impossible journey is the one you never begin." Maybe your journey is writing a book, or maybe it is starting a hobby or a business; know that there are others out there willing to help. Hopefully this story and the ones that follow will encourage you take the first step on your journey to attain your dream and make a difference in others' lives through Everyday Leadership.

CHAPTER 3

LEADERSHIP: A BRIEF HISTORY

I know it when I see it.
—United States Supreme Court
Justice Potter Stewart

In terms of Supreme Court decisions, this quote is one of the most well-known and often recited sentences in history. As time has passed, we often see this sentence used well beyond the court's original intention of defining "hard-core pornography." Today, it is widely used to explain something that we know, can see, and can feel that at the same time is extremely subjective or hard to explain or define.

The concept of "leadership" falls into this category as well. For more than 150 years, scholars have offered opinions, debated, and discussed what leadership is and what makes someone an effective leader.

Many questions are at the heart of these discussions on leadership, often originating from leadership theories combined with an individual's experiences and biases as a leader. Funnily enough, we learn many of our leadership habits from observing others in leadership positions. While most of this book is intended to push your thinking around leadership and provide you concepts and tangible examples of how to become a more effective leader, I strongly believe that to know where you're going, you have to know where you came from. That warrants a brief overview on leadership theory.

Leadership over the Years

In 1840, Thomas Carlyle developed the first modern-day concept around leadership theory called the "great man theory." In his book *On Heroes, Hero-Worship, and the Heroic in History*, Carlyle stated: "The history of the world is but the biography of great men." He identified a number of these great men: people like Muhammad, Shakespeare, Martin Luther, and Napoleon. Carlyle believed great men were born with certain traits; these endowed men (it was 1840, so there was no mention of women) rose to the occasion when needed and were the deciding factor in several historical events.

Twenty-nine years later, Francis Galton in *Hereditary Genius* took Carlyle's idea further. Galton stipulated that leaders had immutable characteristics that could not be developed. This concept, known as the trait theory of leadership, has evolved through the work of Ralph Stogdill in the mid-twentieth century, followed by James Kouzes and Barry Posner, who published *The Leadership*

Challenge in 1987. Like Stogdill, they focused on what traits people wanted in leaders.

Through interviews and surveys, Kouzes and Posner evolved trait theory to say it is an "observable, learnable set of practices"[2] and identified "The Five Practices of Exemplary Leadership," which are "Model the Way," "Inspire a Shared Vision," "Challenge the Status Quo," "Enable Others to Act," and "Encourage the Heart."[3] Trait leadership theory spawned many of today's trait/behavioral assessments including the big five theory, which measures openness, conscientiousness, extraversion, agreeableness, and neuroticism, as well as the Myers-Briggs Type Indicator (see chapter 6: "Old MacDonald Had a Farm E-or-I, E-or-I-Oh…Sh*t"), which tries to help us narrow the traits to better understand ourselves and each other.

Contingency theory is a third theory of leadership. This theory states that positive results are a combination of the situation and leader's style. While there is substantial research around this theory and other spinoffs—Fiedler's theory, situational theory, and decision-making theory (Vroom-Yetton Model)—the general premise of all can best be summarized by Villanova University: "Effective leadership is contingent on the situation, task and people involved."[4]

---

2   Brian Evje, "9 Leadership Myths—& How to Overcome Them," *Lead. Inc.*, Retrieved 7 October 2013.

3   Drake Baer, "What Leaders Do When They're at Their Best," *Fast Company*, Retrieved 7 October 2013.

4   https://www.villanovau.com/resources/leadership/contingency-theory-leadership/

A fourth theory is behavioral leadership theory. "Behavioral leadership theory argues that the success of a leader is based on their behavior rather than their natural attributes. Behavioral leadership theory involves observing and evaluating a leader's actions and behaviors when they are responding to a specific situation. This theory believes that leaders are made, not born. Proponents of this theory suggest that anyone can become an effective leader if they can learn and implement certain behaviors."[5]

While these theories all have credibility and value, they also have significant assumptions and limitations. The biggest limitation is that all have criteria about who can be a "leader" or what is required to be a "leader." For the great man theory, you have to be born with it. With trait theory, it is about figuring out which of the more than 100 potential characteristics drive leadership. While the extraordinary work by Posner and Kouzes has narrowed this down, their focus has traditionally been on leadership in business. With contingency theory, it is about the situation, and with behavioral leadership theory it is all about actions.

To be clear, each of these researchers and corresponding theories have done a tremendous amount to advance the conversation—actually the debate—around leadership. At the same time, these theories have one common

---

5   What is Behavioral Leadership Theory? Definition and Types of Behavioral Leadership | Indeed.com https://www.indeed.com/career-advice/career-development/behavioral-leadership-theory#:~:text=Behavioral%20leadership%20theory%20argues%20that,responding%20to%20a%20specific%20situation.

limitation: their subjective criteria make leadership seem elusive and exclusive, limiting leadership to narrow definitions, characteristics, and situations—which, ironically, is the exact opposite of what leadership should be.

Their subjective criteria make leadership seem elusive and exclusive, limiting leadership to narrow definitions, characteristics, and situations—which, ironically, is the exact opposite of what leadership should be.

So why should we succumb to these limitations and restrict leadership? The truth is that we shouldn't!

Leadership comes in many forms and fashions, and even though you might not be able to define it (like pornography), you know it when you see it or, more often than not, don't see it. So let's take leadership off the pedestal and stop thinking only a handful of people with the right pedigrees or characteristics can achieve it. Let's do everything we can to make leadership inclusive because leadership is everywhere—from the boardroom to the playroom, the ballroom to the classroom, the emergency room to the locker room, and the virtual meeting room and many other rooms. Everyday Leadership opportunities abound.

PART I

COMMUNICATION: IT'S NOT ABOUT YOU

Wise men speak because they have something to say;
Fools speak because they have to say something.
—Plato

From the beginning of time, when our ancestors called caves home, we have worked to communicate with one another. We started with etching images on rocks and over time have used a variety of methods (smoke signals, carrier pigeons, letters, telegraphs, fax machines) to communicate. Now we have many modern-day forms of communication: email, text messages, internet-based tools such as blogs, and social media platforms like Twitter and Facebook. Humanity has constantly worked to develop and push the boundaries of how we communicate with one another.

Interestingly enough, as our options for communication have expanded, our decisions on how we communicate have also become more complex. Now, more than ever, we not only have to choose what to communicate, but must also consider the most effective medium to deliver our message. As the world has expanded around us and our ability to connect is greater than ever before, communication has become even more crucial to our success as human beings.

Humans are social creatures, and we want to connect and communicate with our families and friends. As parents, we have a responsibility not only to communicate effectively with our kids but to teach them effective communication skills, including manners, the importance of speaking and writing confidently, communicating with civility, and the effect of body language and mannerisms on communication. As they mature and grow, we also have a responsibility to help them understand the impact of their own communication decisions, especially on social media.

Apply this concept to modern business, and communication takes on another complicated layer of intricacy, meaning, and challenges. How does one leader or a small group of leaders disseminate their vision, mission, and directives to hundreds if not thousands of team members? How does a small business owner clearly and effectively share her brand and products with her audience? How does a medium-sized company work to create decisive and crystal-clear imperatives that are easy to follow and beneficial to leadership and the overall path of the company?

As you can see, the journey through communication is a complicated series of pushes and pulls, ups and downs, and barriers to entry with a dose of adversity along the way. But for every challenge you face as a leader communicating your message, there is a less tried and more succinct path to reach your goals. To be frank, communication doesn't have to be that hard. However, learning how to communicate isn't particularly easy either.

This section of the book summarizes the lessons learned as I watched others communicate and failed (and occasionally succeeded) at communicating myself. I came to recognize that communication, like anything else, can be much easier and more empowering when you study it and work at improving how you actually do it. For you, the reader, I want communication to be second nature, so you can be an effective communicator who can move your team members to action and reach your goals, whatever they may be. Nothing needs to be lost in communication; rather all can be gained as you communicate.

Together, we embark on an exciting journey, one that will help you understand how you communicate, and offer ideas so you can make any changes needed to be the best communicator you can be. Tony Robbins offers us great insight: "To effectively communicate, we must realize that we are all different in the way we perceive the world and use this understanding as a guide to our communication with others."[6]

The beauty of communicating is that we can create our own path, journey, style, and, of course, directives

---

6   https://www.brainyquote.com/quotes/tony_robbins_132532

for how we share information with others. Once we do so at a high level, and with thoughtful direction, we can move people to action, change lives, and forge a path that lasts, that matters, and that shapes the lives of those around us.

CHAPTER 4

COMMUNICATIONS AND EXPECTATIONS ARE 90% OF SUCCESS

The single biggest problem in communication
is the illusion that it has taken place.
—George Bernard Shaw

In the summer of 2013, I had just led the consolidation and creation of a shared services center and was newly responsible for the work of over 500 team members across dozens of departments. This was both a tremendous risk and opportunity. To set the tone for how I expected us to operate, I held a kick-off meeting where I brought in the top thirty leaders. Some people had been with the organization less than thirty days, while a couple of folks had been with the organization for more than thirty years. After reviewing the agenda, I started the meeting by sharing "Brian's Ways of Working." And at the top of the bulleted list was "Communications and Expectations are 90% of Success."

This was a simple mantra that I had been touting for years after watching people and projects go awry because people failed to communicate effectively, and their outputs differed from what the client or boss was expecting. Hilary (my wife) was also working full-time, managing a contract with the United States Air Force (USAF) to support quality initiatives at 74 facilities in six countries with more than 44,000 medical staff. Her role was all-encompassing and extremely stressful, but it helped the USAF reduce events that could harm patients by 70% in five years.[7] These amazing results improved the medical safety of those who ensure the safety of the United States of America.

While we both were delivering in our professions and found our work tremendously satisfying, our jobs were intense and full of pressure. There were some new people (and in my case new technology as well), but the biggest driver of success for our roles was defining, establishing, and communicating what success looks like at all levels—both to gain buy-in and to measure results. At the end of the day, we were both successful because we could effectively communicate and set expectations for others.

A few months later, on the home front, our son Harris was just starting first grade. One day, the school sent home a list of after-school activities being offered. While he played basketball in the winter and baseball in the spring, we didn't have him playing an organized team sport in the fall. Even so, he did have tennis lessons a

---

7   https://synensysglobal.com/success-stories/usaf-medical-service/

couple of days a week. The after-school activities were very helpful for everyone in the family, especially because our son is a very active kid who loves to be busy and challenged and we were both working full time.

So at dinner that night, where most of our family conversations happen, the three of us reviewed the after-school activities form. We noticed that a ballroom dancing program was scheduled for Mondays. To our surprise, Harris immediately said he was interested.

Even though we had nothing else for him to do, Hilary and I were eyeing each other, thinking that ballroom dancing was probably not going to be a success for anyone involved. Since the form wasn't due for another week, we tabled the discussion and said we would pick it up later in the week.

Meanwhile, Hilary and I discussed the ballroom dancing program and thought it could be a disaster. Even so, we decided if he really wanted to do it then we should sign him up. We figured it was only ten weeks of classes and the footwork might help him in his organized sports and tennis—especially because I was only an average athlete and a terrible dancer. So we signed him up and sent in the check; a few days later he received confirmation of his enrollment in ballroom dancing.

He started ballroom dancing the following week. After that first Monday, we eagerly awaited Harris's impressions. While the three of us were sitting at the dinner table, I asked Harris, "How was your day at school?" He replied, "It was good." If you have or have had a six-year-old, you probably remember that three-word answers are pretty standard at this age. Nevertheless, I probed with a few additional questions that occasionally led to additional information, but typically the conversation was "asked and answered."

So I then asked him, "How was ballroom dancing?" He replied, "It was okay." So I followed up like this:

Question	Answer
"What did you do?" →	"We learned some dances."
"How many kids were there?" →	"I don't know."
"Did you have a partner?" →	"Yes."
"The same one the whole time?" →	"No."

Again, trying to get details from a six-year-old is not the easiest thing to do . . .

We were there as a family at the dinner table the following Monday. Determined, I asked Harris, "How was school?" He answered, "It was good." "How was ballroom dancing?" I asked. He said, "Half of the boys quit."

Hilary and I locked eyes, and we started to explain how:

1. "We don't quit things." We had talked for a long time before signing up, and we had committed to doing this.
2. "The girls are counting on you." Since half of the boys had quit, your participation is even more important. Finally, I appealed to his highly analytical side by saying:

3. "You're 20% of the way done. There are only eight more classes."

Our responses seemed to placate him, and another week found us back at the dinner table on Monday evening. I asked Harris, "How was school?" He answered, "It was good." I followed up with, "How was ballroom dancing?"

He responded with dead silence. He was desperately searching his six-year-old vocabulary for something to say. I looked across the table at Hilary for a sign of which one of us should intervene when he blurted, "It's just not what I was expecting."

So we both looked at him and then at each other. After he looked at his mom and then back at me, I asked the natural question, "What were you expecting?"

Harris stretched his arms out wide from his shoulders and said emphatically, "A big room with a bunch of balls where I could dance."

Immediately, a few thoughts went through my head. First, I felt like the absolute worst parent on the planet. Here I was, someone who for years had touted, heck shouted, that "communications and expectations are 90% of success." And in our own home we had failed our six-year-old. Simultaneously, I thought, *Of course you did. He's never seen Dancing with the Stars, and he didn't have a clue what ballroom dancing was.* Then I went back to thinking about how bad of a parent I was.

Here's a kid who I had described to others as "loves everything with a ball" because of his penchant for sports.

But I could not connect the dots and realize he thought he was signing up for a birthday party like atmosphere with music and a giant plastic ball pit or for dancing like he's at a party with a DJ or band.

We talked about it a little more, but he never asked to quit. He went to each of the next seven sessions, and each Monday evening at dinner he shared with us that ballroom dancing was becoming a little more tolerable.

A recital was held at the end of the ten sessions, and I had never been prouder of Harris. Here's a kid who was doing great academically, had hit home runs on the baseball field, had scored goals in soccer and baskets on the court. But I was proud because he had stuck it out and made the best of something he didn't realize he was signing up for. At the end of the recital, he even had the teacher asking him if he would do it again the following semester, to which he quickly answered, "I don't think so."

The moral of the story is that no matter how good we think we are at communicating, we can always be better. In grad school, I learned that if you separate the letters in the word "assume," you get "ass," "u," and "me," and that's typically what happens when you assume: It does make somebody look foolish…in this case me.

To be an effective Everyday Leader, you must be an outstanding communicator.

Consider this example in the backdrop of your life. Do you communicate clearly with your team at work? Are you giving them precise details and specific actions they can follow? How about at home? If clarity is the grease that keeps the wheel moving, then interpretation

---

To be an effective Everyday Leader, you must be an outstanding communicator.

---

is the pothole that stops it dead in its track. But it doesn't have to be that way if you stop worrying about the grease and start thinking about the potholes. Work every single day to fill the potholes of communication, knowing that they might be the reason a simple task turns into a complicated dance…or series of dance classes.

PERSPECTIVES WHEREFROM GRANDPARENT TEAM
UNDERSTAND BUSINESS EXECUTIVE LOCKER ROOM
TOGETHER HELP OTHERS HOBBIES EMPOWERING
SOLVE MORE PROBLEMS THAN YOU CAUSE IMPROVE
COMMUNICATION CANDID THINK DIFFERENTLY
TOWARDS THE FUTURE BELIEVE POSITIVE INTENT
INCREASE YOUR KNOWLEDGE BEST SELF-AWARE
INTEGRITY WORKING HARD AND CLARITY
RELATIONSHIPS GROWTH MINDSET GENUINE HUMBLE
SEPARATE FACTS FROM FICTION EXPECTATIONS
TEACHER FAILURE IS NECESSARY CONNECT THE DOTS

CHAPTER 5

PEANUT BUTTER AND JELLY

We are all different in the way we perceive the world. We must use this understanding as a guide to our communication with others.
—Tony Robbins

What do making a delicious peanut butter and jelly sandwich and leadership have in common? You might think these two concepts couldn't possibly relate to each other, but you would be completely mistaken. My affection for PB&Js started much earlier than my interest in leadership. In fact, in the mid-1990s, a significant amount of my sustenance consisted of the giant containers of peanut butter and jelly (and the sliced white bread) available twenty-four/seven in my fraternity house. Breakfast? PB&J. Lunch? PB&J. Dinner? PB&J. Snack? PB&J. Late-night munchies? PB&J. No doubt, whatever the time, it was PB&J.

I am not quite sure where I would be without this wonderful delicacy. Now, you might think the process of creating a delicious PB&J is foolproof, but that is where you are mistaken. You need three separate items to create peanut butter and jelly sandwiches. While we all know (or at least think we know) how to make a peanut butter and jelly sandwich, have you ever written down the steps it takes to create this masterpiece? Try it on for size.

Take just five to ten minutes to write down all the steps required to make a peanut butter and jelly sandwich. Then give these written directions to a family member or a roommate. Even if they know exactly how to make this time-tested sandwich, ask them to set their knowledge aside and follow the directions exactly. Have them follow your step-by-step instructions, without using any knowledge other than what's on your list. Chances are the instructions you wrote, if followed word for word, probably will not create a traditional example of a peanut butter and jelly sandwich.

Now, what does that have to do with leadership? Bear with me here. When asked to conduct leadership training, I often use this process to show the importance of clear communication. Time and time again, I repeat this exercise with hundreds of people. I ask them to write down the instructions, and after collecting their work I try to follow the steps they laid out right there in front of them. Only a few times has someone written instructions creating something that actually resembles a peanut butter and jelly sandwich. Why is that? Well, because the author typically presumes that I know the basics and leaves out vital steps.

The point of the exercise is to demonstrate how we skip steps that we think other people inherently might know. Or to say it another way—we assume they know. For example, I often find that the instructions fail to tell the chef to open the bag of bread and the jar of peanut butter before putting the "peanut butter on the bread." They don't detail which side of the bread to use. Remember, a slice of bread has two large sides, but it also has four more sides encompassed in crust. Most people assume that one would use a knife or other appropriate kitchen utensil to remove the peanut butter from the jar. But if there is no detail regarding this step, I might just use my hands to scoop it out and put it on the bread. Fun, but not effective.

In this example, we see how telling someone to make something so simple as a peanut butter and jelly sandwich can easily lead to a breakdown in communication or at worst complete systems failure. We can then easily understand how any human intensive (aka "human middleware") process can have low reliability for both repeatability (the same person taking the same action over and over in the same situation) and replicability (two people doing the exact same job the same way given identical circumstances).

How can the instructions be improved? Two ways.

In my experience, the first improvement happened as an accident when I gave participants the choice to work alone or with a partner. I did this as a timesaver, because I would not have had enough time to make all of the PB&J

sandwiches if everyone wrote instructions. And what did those who partnered up create? Instructions that were much clearer. Having someone else on your team to hear and see what you are doing and give real-time feedback created additional clarity in the instructions.

A second way the directions were improved was by creating "IKEA-like" instructions. If you have never put together a piece of IKEA furniture, you should know their instructions have no words, just pictures—yes, universal, egalitarian instructions that can be read in any language because there are no words.

Now, apply this concept to leadership communication. Leaders regularly communicate a process or a task to team members. Often they do so incompletely. They then wonder, perhaps are even shocked, when the result is much different than their vision. Leaders look at their teams, start pointing fingers, and remain dumbfounded about why their metaphorical peanut butter and jelly sandwich looks primed to be such a categorical failure. In reality, they should be looking in the mirror at the deliverer of the instructions, not the receivers.

So how did I make sure we were all making PB&J sandwiches? Frequently, I had others review and read communications to ensure they conveyed my intended message clearly. It is why I sought a coach for this book; I don't want to waste your time with a bunch of unnecessary words or incomplete

Yes, I left the last sentence open on purpose to demonstrate my point: it's easy to omit a word or miss your point. Ironically, those who think they are great communicators can be some of the worst because they don't think to circle back to ensure clarity.

Even definitions of the same word can lead people astray. I remember when one of my consulting clients was merging several different companies. There were professional services companies and others that performed tasks and transactions. Early in the integration process, one senior leader (who happened to be from the professional services side) led a town hall. The session was extremely well done, providing an update to the top 100 people across the portfolio of companies.

At one point during the town hall, the senior leader stated that "back-office operations were going to be consolidated." The person meant that functions such as HR, finance, purchasing, and IT would be brought together. While all the leaders from the professional services side knew exactly what was being communicated, some leaders from other companies who provided outsourcing services referred to the tasks of their companies and teams as "operations." They were immediately concerned for their jobs and livelihoods because of what they considered an impending consolidation.

Who would've thought the word "operations" could cause a problem?

For another part of my consulting business, I provide insights to large consulting firms, private equity companies, venture capitalists, and other investors on the state of health care, more specifically on companies with solutions for improving the administrative and financial side of health care. I always start those calls by saying, 'I don't want to be presumptive or condescending, so please give me feedback if you need more details or tell me to speed up if you already know what I'm saying.'

On the home front, no so long ago, we were potty training our two-and-a-half-year-old daughter, Sara. The concept of sitting on the potty is a jungle (more about jungles later in the book) for a toddler. She was still going in her pull-up about half the time. I said to her, "We need to do a better job getting you on the potty more often." She responded, "Not a sick job." In her

---

I don't want to be presumptive or condescending, so please give me feedback if you need more details or tell me to speed up if you already know what I'm saying.

---

mind, if you are sick, you get better. She took my word "better" in her definition. This was a learning moment for me and her. The English language is hard.

While you may not be consulting or potty training, here's a great tip for meetings or conference calls: save time at the end for a recap, when you can review what was decided and list any action items with owners and due dates. It sounds simple, but more than half the time someone will seek clarification on something during the recap, even though they did not ask about it when the task was originally assigned or taken.

So next time you're trying to explain something to someone, think about whether your description and information really are detailed and comprehensive enough to generate success. That is not the case on most occasions. In fact, we naturally presume that others know what we are thinking or can readily fill in the blanks. In reality, the opposite is likely more accurate. As human beings, we appreciate and even need details and direction. If you are looking for a creative exercise or interpretation, it is perfectly acceptable to allow those receiving your directions to create their own metaphorical sandwiches. But, if you are looking for a specific outcome, like a delicious PB&J, it is crucial that you constantly communicate in a way that gives your team members the steps they need to complete the assigned task.

PERSPECTIVES WHEREFROM GRANDPARENT TEAM
UNDERSTAND BUSINESS EXECUTIVE LOCKER ROOM
TOGETHER HELP OTHERS HOBBIES EMPOWERING
SOLVE MORE PROBLEMS THAN YOU CAUSE IMPROVE
COMMUNICATION CANDID THINK DIFFERENTLY
TOWARDS THE FUTURE BELIEVE POSITIVE INTENT
INCREASE YOUR KNOWLEDGE BEST SELF-AWARE
INTEGRITY CLARITY
RELATIONSHIPS GROWTH MINDSET GENUINE HUMBLE
SEPARATE CTATIONS
TEACHER FAILURE IS NECESSARY CONNECT THE DOTS

CHAPTER 6

OLD MACDONALD HAD A FARM E-OR-I, E-OR-I-OH...SH*T

Leadership is all about people. It is not about organizations. It is not about plans. It is not about strategies. It is all about people-motivating people to get the job done. You have to be people-centered.
—Colin Powell

While evangelizing the notion that "communications and expectations are 90% of success," I have constantly searched for new tools and ways to improve communication with those around me, including the teams I lead. At one point in my career, I was tasked with leading a massive transformation effort. To succeed, we needed some dedicated resources to lead various components of the business. One of our internal leaders seemed like a perfect fit. She had knowledge (over twenty-five years in the industry), experience in the organization (about a decade), and respect (from her peers, her boss, subordinates, physicians, and other stakeholders). She had identified opportunities for improvement and best practices, and if that wasn't enough, she was looking to do something different and grow her career.

Given all these facts, I thought she was the perfect person to lead the transformation for a specific group of functions for the future of our entire health system. When she joined the team, I told her we needed her to develop our future operations. A few weeks later we got back together, and I was surprised with her output, or rather lack thereof. She brought me a mix of principles she wanted to have and goals she wanted to achieve, but mostly she just had a list that started a conversation around the tactics and results she expected to accomplish. What she brought was not bad, but it wasn't a strategy or plan to get us from our current state to a future one.

While I was not upset, I was confused and somewhat dismayed. How could this individual with so much knowledge, experience, insight, and potential not pull together a basic strategy for my review? As a result, we spent more time together (along with some support from outside consultants) to define the future state, identify the gaps and changes, and develop a vision and an overall plan (resources, timing, etc.). I was frustrated because I just could not understand why I needed to spend so much time with someone who had so much knowledge and experience. Once we got through the strategy and future state design, this leader executed the plan flawlessly. She was an operational dynamo who used her knowledge, experience, and relationships to successfully transform the key functions on which we had focused.

Once we completed the task at hand and were stabilized, I started working with our internal learning and development team to formulate a plan for enhancing leadership skills across the division. The first tool we decided to implement was the Myers-Briggs Type Indicator (MBTI). To be clear, this was not a revolutionary decision, as 88% of Fortune 500 companies and 115 countries use Myers-Briggs.[8] In fact, there are hundreds of books on this topic. I am not going to go into great detail, but I do believe an overview will help you and your team members understand your natural inclinations in four areas of personality[9]:

1. How do you direct and receive energy—by focusing on the outside world, interacting with people and taking action, or by focusing on your inner world and reflecting on ideas, memories, and experiences? (**E**xtroversion or **I**ntroversion)

2. How do you take in information—by focusing on what you perceive using your five senses or by seeing the big picture and looking for relationships and patterns? (**S**ensing or i**N**tuition)

3. How do you come to conclusions—by logically analyzing the situation or by considering what is important to the people involved? (**T**hinking or **F**eeling)

---

8   https://www.themyersbriggs.com/en-US/Products-and-Services/Myers-Briggs
9   https://www.themyersbriggs.com/en-US/Products-and-Services/Myers-Briggs

4. How do you approach the outside world—in a planned, orderly way or a more flexible, spontaneous way? (**J**udging or **P**erceiving)

According to the Myers-Briggs website, "Your natural preferences in these four areas sort you into one of 16 distinct MBTI personality types. Understanding these types gives you objective insight that you can use to enhance your professional and personal relationships, as well as your direction, focus, and choices."

The great thing about the MBTI is that there is no wrong answer! Yes, it's an assessment, but it doesn't try to compare you with other people. Instead, it allows you to learn about yourself and others to learn about you. While it identifies a specific type, it shows a continuum where you land; for example, you may be a *strong* Extrovert or a *mild* Extrovert.

For example, I am an ESTJ—Extrovert, Sensing, Thinking, Judging. ESTJs are typically described as people who are efficient, dependable, outgoing, realistic, and analytical; they like things to be done in a predictable, logical way. When others don't take a logical approach to solve a problem, their natural tendency is to try to put one in place to align expectations (sound familiar)[10]. So yes, it describes me pretty well.

Like all the types, ESTJs have strengths like integrity, stewardship, and the ability to create order out of chaos, and they remain dedicated and committed. At the same time, all the types have weaknesses, and ESTJs can be

---

10 https://www.truity.com/personality-type/ESTJ/strengths-weaknesses

judgmental, inflexible or even stubborn, workaholics, and uncomfortable with their emotions—things I constantly must be aware of and work on.[11]

From this exercise I learned that the colleague I mentioned a few paragraphs ago is an ISTJ—Introvert, Sensing, Thinking, Judging. And ISTJs can be summarized as people who "get sh*t done." More completely, the website Truity.com states:

> "ISTJs like to know what the rules of the game are, valuing predictability more than imagination. They rely on their past experience to guide them and are most comfortable in familiar surroundings. ISTJs trust the proven method and appreciate the value of dedicated practice to build confidence in their skills.
>
> ISTJs are hardworking and will persist until a task is done. They are logical and methodical, and often enjoy tasks that require them to use step-by-step reasoning to solve a problem. They are meticulous in their attention to details and examine things closely to be sure they are correct. With their straightforward logic and orientation to detail, ISTJs work systematically to bring order to their own small parts of the world."[12]

So I started reflecting back to the beginning of the transformation and determined that I had chosen someone for a new role who:

---

11 https://www.truity.com/personality-type/ESTJ/strengths-weaknesses
12 https://www.truity.com/personality-type/ISTJ

1. Likes familiar surroundings. But I put her into a new office in a different building with a different team.
2. Likes to know where she stands and the rules of the game. But I asked her to use her imagination to develop a strategy and plan.
3. Likes the proven method. But I asked her not only to figure out the future method but to create a gap analysis and change the management plan to move from the proven method to something completely unproven.

I felt terrible. I thought I was being a terrific leader by giving someone a unique opportunity to show off her skills. Instead, I put her in probably the worst situation possible. I put this incredibly talented, dedicated, conscientious, hardworking, high-integrity person into a situation that set her up for failure. It was clear why I was frustrated, and I realized she was probably even more frustrated with me as a leader. My expectations were clearly inappropriate and unrealistic. After further contemplation, I scheduled a meeting with my colleague and explained to her what I had come to understand. I also apologized to her. Because she was and still is a team player, she shrugged it off and said it didn't bother her. In fact, she inappropriately took the blame, which is a weakness of an ISTJ.

Though she may have forgotten this experience, I never will. You might think that I should have used the MBTI to choose a different person, but that is not the case. For numerous reasons, this leader was far and away the best person for the role.

Instead, I learned the importance of being proactive and using available tools to gain alignment, minimize frustration, and improve productivity. Specifically, with earlier access to the MBTI information, I could have spent more time trying to understand strengths, weaknesses, and natural tendencies when we were first discussing the role.

I thought I was being a terrific leader by giving someone a unique opportunity to show off her skills. Instead, I put her in probably the worst situation possible.

The MBTI is just one way of understanding these traits and using that knowledge in a nonthreatening—actually supportive—way. But other tools can also give you insights into your team or the candidates you might hire or assign to a new role or project. Once you have this information, you can identify the gaps and assess whether they are wide enough to require an intervention...at that point. Whether you choose to intervene or not, you will be more informed and that alone should reduce frustration, improve your likelihood of success, and expand your practice of Everyday Leadership.

CHAPTER 7

REMOVE SUBJECTIVE TERMS FROM YOUR VOCABULARY

*I could have never been a high diver or a gymnast because
I don't like subjectivity. I love where I'm faster than you,
or I can jump higher or swim faster. I don't want you
holding a card before I figure out whether I won or lost.*
—Shannon Sharpe

A
s you now see from my example in chapter 4:
"Communications and Expectations Are 90% of
Success," communication isn't easy. As we assume that
people receiving our directions understand them cor-
rectly and can interpret our goals, we often fail to get
from point A to point B. But failures in communication
don't occur only from a lack of direction. It can also result
from word choice and the terms used when outlining a
task or a responsibility. For example, subjective terms
are great for telling stories but terrible when you want
to effectively communicate anything other than a story.

I have learned that using subjective terms in workplace communications can create numerous unintended challenges. I will give you some examples for insight into why you should avoid subjective terms in workplace communications. But before I get to those examples, I always like to use the example of planning for dinner. Imagine it is 5:00 p.m. I'm still at work, winding down my day, and I reach out to my wife. We chat for a few minutes about our dinner plans. As we close the conversation, I tell her, "I'm going to be leaving the office soon." In this case, the word "soon" is quite subjective. If she thinks "soon" is twenty minutes and I think "soon" is an hour, one of us might end up being very hungry or the food might end up being very cold. Fortunately, that hasn't happened to us...very often. But it demonstrates just how easily one subjective term can completely derail an entire exchange.

Unfortunately, I encounter subjective terms almost daily in the workplace. While working for a large health care organization, I oversaw a team of 1,500, approximately 1,300 people spread across a dozen company-owned locations, along with about 200 more who worked from home. In total, they performed tens of millions of transactions on millions of patient accounts annually. During that time, someone would stop by my office and share that we had a "big problem" or send an email indicating "there are lots of impacted accounts" or mention in a meeting that "an insurance company isn't paying timely." The good news is that these messages rarely, if ever, came from my direct reports. In fact, because of our culture, my direct reports were quick to separate fact from fairy tale. They would first figure out and quantify what "big," "lots," and "timely" meant. While the employees always had our best interests in mind, they might have presumed that an issue was a "big" one when it was, in reality, a very "small" line item for a $3.5 billion business. That said, subjective adjectives can at times take on a life of their own, needlessly consuming untold amounts of resources in operations, analytics, quality assurance, and process improvement.

When we were implementing an electronic medical record system, I would frequently hear outstanding tasks were "almost done" and would be completed "soon." In a complex, interdependent environment, uncertain completion dates and timings for these tasks could impact other tasks and ultimately the go-live date. Repeatedly, I would publicly ask what "almost done" and "soon" meant. I just didn't know how those terms translated into dates on the calendar. Eventually, team members would catch themselves when communicating and would try to quantify (to the best of their ability) the temporal elements around their system build.

Subjective terms come up not just when communicating inside a company but with vendors and partners as well. I was facilitating a session with a vendor and another division in our company to resolve issues and discuss ways to improve the relationship. Despite the challenges, both sides agreed they wanted to continue working together, so we had a meeting. After kicking it off and setting expectations, I backed away since the meeting was going really well. In fact, both sides agreed on several things, including the fact that we needed to schedule "regular meetings" and the "executives should be engaged" moving forward.

As the meeting wrapped up and everyone felt really good, I said to the other four people — two from the vendor and two internal leaders — "What do you all mean by 'regular' when you agreed to have regular meetings?" Simultaneously one group said "quarterly" and the other said "monthly." They ended up agreeing on monthly meetings. Relieved that they solved that issue, they were about to leave and then I asked: "What do you mean by 'executives need to be engaged'?" I had already proven my point, but both sides put down their bags looked at each other and began to clarify the subjective terms they had unintentionally agreed upon. They were simple words that everyone had defined differently.

While they seem harmless, "subjective" terms can create a number of challenges in our personal and professional lives. These careless word choices create gaps in understanding. In the end they can lead to lost time and revenue, unfulfilled expectations, or simply a disconnect in communication of our intentions. In the land of fairy tales and storytelling, subjective terms take us to far-off places and deep, dark crevices. But in the world of fast-moving and low-margin-of-error operations, they are objectively a huge problem. (Yes, I had to use one more subjective term to prove my point.)

CHAPTER 8

RIGHT VERSUS CORRECT

Experience is merely the name men gave to their mistakes.
—Oscar Wilde

This chapters continues to discuss the importance of communication. In it, I want to share another experience, or bad decision, that teaches a great lesson we can all apply to our quest for Everyday Leadership. It happened in the early 2000s when I was in my late twenties, a couple of years into my consulting career. My client was an academic medical center in a major American city. We were supporting and working to improve their revenue cycle.

Like any academic medical center, they were doing a lot to meet their triple aim of education, research, and patient care. To help with this effort, the organization was implementing an electronic medical record system, which was independent of the work we were doing.

A few weeks after turning on the new system, the organization realized it had some issues with recurring accounts (patients who had multiple visits for things like physical therapy, occupational therapy, speech therapy, etc.). In the crazy world of health care billing, many insurance companies want all those visits submitted on a single claim form each month. As a result, the designer should have created a system that supported this business requirement, but the designer hadn't. The business should have then trained the team members to work toward this goal, but it didn't do that either.

This led to approximately 28,000 visits having been incorrectly registered. As a result, these visits could not be billed. Since each visit had a value of more than $85, this became a top priority for the health system and its relatively new CFO. To deal with reregistering, billing, and collecting this approximately $2.4 million opportunity, the CFO asked for our help. My boss assigned me to the project.

This multifaceted project featured the following: cleaning up the existing records (which became my new responsibility), modifying the IT system build, the policies and procedures, and creating a plan to (re) train the dozens of team members across the organization responsible for scheduling and registering these patients. It sounds simple, but a job is never as simple as it seems. Patients with therapy visits typically have other appointments as well, creating lots of options that can lead to incorrect linking and combining of accounts in the system. So separate teams focused on each of these areas, and the CFO had the team leads (including myself as the lead of cleanup) meet every day at 5:00 p.m.

The CFO was super sharp with lots of experience in finance, most recently as a leader at a multinational company that produced consumer household products.

While super smart, she had limited experience in health care and struggled to understand the complexities that existed when humans and technology were forced to interact in thousands of independent but not mutually exclusive events each day.

The cleanup team was a true melting pot of individuals. We had three separate groups:

- **Employees of the health system.** These team members were from various age groups and family situations. Some had been with the health system for a long time and were talented employees with the knowledge and skills to complete the work, but others were assigned because department managers leveraged an opportunity to push marginal employees off their teams.

- **Recent new hires from the medical records vendor.** When I say new hire, I mean someone fresh out of college—newly minted undergraduates. Some had not even fully completed orientation at the medical records vendor. These young and excited rookies came from various parts of the country and were getting their first experience in the "real world." Some had never been to a major U.S. city. They were book smart and sometimes street smart, but most had little to no knowledge of health care. They had taken a job with a technology company and were thrust into solving a client's problem where they were traveling each week and responsible for performing data entry work.

- **Mercenaries.** These were the professional cleanup or fix-it folks. They all had significant experience and traveled from across the country for two weeks at a time to resolve all the accounts.

While this relatively short-term effort lasted only a few months, I learned so much about people, especially because I worked with people from different generations, different parts of the country, different socioeconomic situations, different educational backgrounds, and different life experiences…all packed into a classroom (this was an academic medical center) with desks where they worked on this singular problem.

I chose a member of my team (we will call him N.J.) to direct the hour-by-hour work of these three groups. We needed to find a way to bring them together as a unit. N.J. was and still is a highly intelligent, super analytical, extremely curious, hardworking individual who had earned my trust from our joint work on previous engagements. He rolled up his sleeves to get into the details and would do anything and everything that he would ask anyone else to do. He has a disarming, self-deprecating personality and could relate to everyone. Looking back, he was often the secret ingredient, whether he knew it or not, that pulled these individuals together into a team.

This team worked hard day in and day out to execute our plan and ensure that the health care system received accurate payments for the services it provided. Every workday, I would check in with N.J. and the team so I could obtain the status on resolving the 28,000 encounters. We would review progress, go over issues, identify solutions, communicate with the team, and celebrate milestones. I would then summarize these items and trek to the 5:00 p.m. meeting.

The CFO led this daily meeting, and the team members representing the different aspects of the remediation effort would give their updates. Besides myself, IT and operations leaders were present, all of whom were more than a decade older than me. Yes, I was the one who didn't belong—the consultant, the outsider, and the kid. I did not have much of a relationship with these people. My work was segmented, and the fact that I was a consultant and not an employee created tension.

While the cleanup was going well, other parts of the project were having some challenges making progress. And the CFO wanted progress. To help improve the tenor of the meetings, I started connecting with each person giving updates. I quickly realized they were not making progress because they spent almost half of their day preparing for the 5:00 p.m. meeting. They were spending just as much time working to give an update as they were to solve the problem. It just seemed odd and nonproductive. As a result, I decided I would let the CFO know what I had observed and then recommend a different approach. After all, I was a consultant who they were paying to do exactly that.

So that afternoon, I went to the daily 5:00 p.m. beating, I mean *meeting*, and as it was closing, the CFO asked, "Does anyone have anything else to discuss?" So I said something to the effect of "I have observed that the other people in this room are spending half of their day preparing for this meeting. This takes their time away from making progress on the effort and just increases the questions you have as well as the time to get the work done. So I suggest having this meeting only two or three days each week."

At this point, fire lit up the CFO's eyes. She stood up and put her hands firmly on the table, slowly looking around to make eye contact with everyone individually before saying, "I will see you here at 5:00 p.m. tomorrow." With that, she abruptly walked out.

The other people in the room, whom I had very little relationship with, immediately thanked me for trying and "taking one for the team." I had not intended to use this as an opportunity to make new friends. I was just trying to do the right thing for them and save time for all of us. It was as if they finally realized I was actually trying to help them.

Obviously, I was disappointed the CFO didn't give my recommendation any consideration. That said, I went to bed knowing in my heart I was trying to do the right thing. The next morning, I woke up and was on my way to the client's site when my Nokia cell phone started lighting up like the Christmas tree at Rockefeller Center.

First it was the partner who was leading the engagement. He told me he had heard the CFO was extremely unhappy and would talk to me when I got to the client's site. Then I received a call from the partner who managed the relationship with the client. As I answered the phone, I thought for sure I was going to be fired. On the other end of the line spoke Frank Paterno.

You see, for Frank (or anyone for that matter) to have become a partner at a major consulting firm, he had to be really good at what he did. Frank was terrific at relating to people. I only saw him about once a week when he came to meet with the client (or maybe a second time when he put together a team event at one of his favorite places). I clearly remember that all activity pretty much stopped when Frank entered our consulting team room. It was as if the president had walked in. Frank was not the president, but he was a presence—a presence that had positional power and everyone's respect. As a team, we all worked really hard to make sure the client was getting results and that Frank had the information he needed to ensure those results as well as making sure issues and opportunities were communicated to the client's executive leadership.

To do this, we would create huge PowerPoint presentations and Excel spreadsheets. Bill Gates would have been proud to see his software being used to generate such material. By the amount of work we produced, you would have thought we were getting paid by the pound of paper we were creating.

Frank was an "old school" partner. I vividly remember him on his laptop, "pecking" a response to an email one key at a time. In fact, Frank and I seemed to be completely different. We were from different generations and had significantly different life experiences. He was the life of the party, whereas I was more reserved. In addition, I was at the very bottom of the consulting hierarchy and was based out of a different office. As a result, I didn't have much of a relationship with Frank. But a couple of months before my fateful decision to offer my opinion to the CFO, I had my only meaningful interaction with Frank, up to that point...

For some reason—probably because one of the more senior people was out—I worked for a few days putting together a summary of the approximately one dozen initiatives for Frank's meeting with client executives. I had created these summaries from each of the team's status reports and presentations to the middle management, as well as conversations with our team leaders. I worked hard on the summaries and was so proud that I had consolidated dozens of pages from the myriad of sources into about fifteen pages that told the whole story.

When Frank arrived that afternoon, I was still working on the update. But it was 99% done...so I was close. To ensure Frank was up to speed on what I had prepared for him, we met, and I walked him through the updates. He was listening to me and flipping back and forth between the pages in the deck. About ten minutes into what I thought was a thirty-minute update and preparation session, I had covered the highlights but was about to get into the details. He then stopped me and said, "I have what I need." He ripped one page out of the deck and asked if I could make him some copies or printouts of it.

Frank's action of taking just the one page shocked me—one page that would have taken less than an hour to create versus all the work I had spent days pulling together. But Frank was the boss, so I did what the boss asked. Frank left and I was dismayed, wondering if I had just wasted days working on something unnecessary.

After the meeting, Frank stopped back by our consulting team room and came over to tell me the meeting had gone well. He described numerous key points I had either shared verbally or written on the other slides he didn't take with him. He then thanked me for all of my efforts. Frank's action of coming back to spend a few minutes did wonders for me personally. I went from wondering if I had wasted my time and questioning myself about what I could have done better, or more importantly could do better next time, to knowing that I had actually done a good job.

This had meant a lot to me at the time, and while I was hoping Frank would take my previous work into account, it was a new day. In consulting, you're only as good as your most recent interaction/meeting—and based on my meeting from the previous day, I still thought I was about to be fired.

Frank started our conversation by saying, "Good morning, Brian. It's Frank Paterno," as if the caller ID on my phone didn't work and I needed to be reminded who he was. Frank went on to say, "I got a call last night from the CFO who shared what happened in the meeting yesterday at 5:00 p.m." At this point, I was expecting Frank to say that I should pack my bags. Instead, Frank said, "Tell me what happened." I explained the situation exactly as I explained it in this book. Afterward, he concurred that the CFO had said the same thing, and then he profoundly stated in a measured pace and tone, "You were right, but you weren't correct."

Frank went on to explain how the message I conveyed was absolutely right, but the *way* I conveyed the message was wrong. He said, "The CFO felt as if you were trying to show her up and put her on the spot because you did it in a public setting with others who were directly impacted in the room." He went on to add, "You would have definitely gotten a better response if you would have asked for a few minutes with the CFO at the end of the meeting where you could share your idea one-on-one."

I was rapidly trying to digest this insightful information (still thinking I was going to be fired) when he added, "But even if you did it in a one-on-one setting, it probably wouldn't have been received that well because you don't have a relationship with the CFO." Then he provided further insights, saying, "I do have a relationship and I am the one who would have been more than happy to deliver that message for you and will do so in the future."

My mind was all over the place, but I realized that he had just said the word "future." That meant I might not be getting fired after all. It turns out I didn't get fired, but I did have a more experienced/senior manager from the firm join me at the daily 5:00 p.m. huddle for the next two weeks. After this, the CFO told the group we would be reducing the meeting frequency to twice in-person each week and a call on Fridays.

People say the road to hell is paved with good intentions, and I thought mine was as well. But Frank's leadership and trust in me—or should I say trust in my intentions—led him to use this opportunity as a teaching and coaching moment. Frank had every reason and right to be extremely upset, but he displayed Everyday Leadership instead. Frank's leadership and investment in me made a tremendously positive impact on my career, and I have in turn shared the story as well as his guidance with others.

To go from right to correct and to ensure successful communications, you need to realize the communication is not about you, it's about the person or people you are communicating to. Evaluate these elements to ensure successful communications every day, every time:

- **People:** Who is the right person to communicate the message to your audience?
- **Place:** Where should the message be communicated?
- **Context:** What are the circumstances around the message?
- **Message:** Is the message simply informative, or does it require a response or further communication?
- **Mechanism:** Should it take place in person, on the phone, via email, text, or fax?
- **Tone:** Is the message likely to be well received, or is it something someone does not want to learn?
- **Timing:** When is the best time to communicate?

You need to realize the communication is not about you, it's about the person or people you are communicating to.

When you evaluate these elements and factor each into your communications, you might recognize that any opportunity to be "right" but not "correct" is not an opportunity at all. For most, communication is not just in the message but also in the delivery and timing. I was 100% right in my assessment of the problem, but my approach was 100% wrong. That occurs on many occasions: right message, wrong approach. As you work to improve your communicative skills moving forward, factor in the ol' lesson my mentor Frank taught me. You can be right but not correct.

PERSPECTIVES WHEREFROM GRANDPARENT TEAM
UNDERSTAND BUSINESS EXECUTIVE LOCKER ROOM
TOGETHER HELP OTHERS HOBBIES EMPOWERING
SOLVE MORE PROBLEMS THAN YOU CAUSE IMPROVE
COMMUNICATION CANDID THINK DIFFERENTLY
TOWARDS THE FUTURE BELIEVE POSITIVE INTENT
INCREASE YOUR KNOWLEDGE BEST SELF-AWARE
INTEGRITY WORDS CLARITY
RELATIONSHIPS GROWTH MINDSET GENUINE HUMBLE
SEPARATE FACTS FROM FAIRY TALES EXPECTATIONS
TEACHER FAILURE IS NECESSARY CONNECT THE DOTS

CHAPTER 9

WORDS MATTER

If you want to be happy, set a goal that commands your thoughts, liberates your energy, and inspires your hopes.
—Andrew Carnegie

My last name, Unell, is unusual (and if you are wondering, it is pronounced You-nell). As a result, I routinely get questions about its origin. According to Ancestry.com, my great grandparents (Unell) were born in Russia and my grandfather was born in Missouri. My dad's parents moved to Atlanta from St. Louis in the mid-1940s with my aunt, who was a toddler, and little more than the promise of a job for my grandfather. Shortly afterward, my father was born in Atlanta. Several years later, my grandparents started a business called Atlanta Thread & Supply. For the next four decades, my grandfather traveled the southeast selling buttons, thread, and sewing supplies to tailors. They sold the business in the late 1980s, and in the early 2000s the company was again sold to a larger thread and supply company called Wawak.

My grandparents lived a very modest lifestyle but were generous with their time and to their family. One day when I was around eight years old, I clearly remember my grandfather saying, "With a name like Unell, you don't want to end up on the front page of the *Atlanta Journal.*" (That was the name of Atlanta's afternoon newspaper before it merged with the *Atlanta Constitution*).

For almost forty years, that quote has stuck with me and has helped guide my decision-making framework: I do my best to stay off the front page of our local newspaper. In February 1996, my mom's mom and my dad's

---

"With a name like Unell, you don't want to end up on the front page of the *Atlanta Journal.*"

---

dad passed away a few days apart. Obviously, it was a sad time for our family, but at the same time we recognized and were grateful for the fact that they had lived well. Immediately after my grandfather's funeral, I remember sitting at the cemetery in the special white folding chair that only cemeteries seem to have when the son of a long-time friend of my grandparents came up to me and said, "Your grandfather was a good man."

At that time, I said to myself that there is no better compliment than that. I also vowed that I was going to do everything I could in life so that when I passed, someone would share the same words about me.

Fast-forward about twenty years later—I bought one suit and "got three free" at Joseph A. Banks. While I was getting the suit measured, I noticed that the gentleman had a ruler that said, "Atlanta Thread & Supply." I shared with him that my grandparents had started the company. He then picked up my order and looked at the last name with an expression of shock. He went on to tell me how well he knew my grandfather, making sure to inform me that his reputation within the industry was second to none and how good of a person and businessman he had been.

About the same time, I requested an executive coach and a 360 feedback survey in which I asked more than thirty-five people to provide their thoughts about my strengths as well as areas of opportunity. My boss asked me, "Are you sure you want a 360 feedback?" The culture in the company then, as well as in many others, was that 360 feedbacks were for people who were not performing well. But because I was in a new role—my first executive role with lots of different customers and stakeholders—I believed the feedback was necessary to help me identify trends so I could improve my leadership skills. I also wanted to set the tone that I really was open to feedback from everyone.

The survey was 100% anonymous and included dozens of *"Please rate the individual on a scale from 1 to 5"* questions followed by one open ended question:

> *Considering the person's total performance and contribution to the organization, what do you think is this*

person's single greatest strength, and what do you think is the one improvement area that, if met, would have the greatest impact on this person's performance?

While almost all the comments were constructive, one person shared the following...

"Hopefully this is confidential but Brian has one of the lowest levels of emotional intelligence I have encountered in a large organization. Brian is the bad leader that everyone had either in sports, college or the military.

He builds silos, has no respect for healthy dissent, or other views. If Brian is not gone within three months you will have a move towards the door of some talented people."

I don't know who wrote it, and I never will but the person knew me well enough to push the buttons that would reach, actually puncture, the core of who I am and my values. While it was just one of more than 30 other (constructive) comments, it was extremely painful to read, especially the part about being a "bad leader in sports" because I was coaching my son's kindergarten basketball team at the time.

Not only did I stay more than three months, but over the next seven years, my division became a talent magnet for leadership, attracting some of the best revenue cycle operators in the region. For example, one day a few years later, a colleague from another local health system called to tell me that she encouraged her 20+ year protégé to come work with me. To this day, receiving that phone call was one of the most humbling moments of my career and best compliments I have ever received. But it was more than an outlier; department wide our annual turnover went from the national average of 20%-25% to less than 10% during the last two years of my tenure. If I had a working crystal ball that could have predicted these results, the destructive personal attack from the 360 feedback would have had less impact but in the moment the comment was debilitating and all consuming.

The days, weeks, months, and years that followed the 360 feedback included many nights each week where I went to bed and mornings when I woke up thinking about the comment; wondering who and why someone would go out of their way to intentionally inflict so much pain when all I am trying to do is to make myself a better leader?

Over the next few years, 360 feedback assessments became more prevalent across the organization. I went through a second assessment, and it showed tremendous personal and professional growth. Nevertheless, knowing firsthand how much the negative comment impacted me and seeing the impact of these anonymous comments on my colleagues, I decided that I was not going to provide anonymous feedback to anyone anymore. Specifically, when presented with the privilege, responsibility, and opportunity to provide 360 feedback, I always ended my comments with my initials and offered up my time to provide further insights or perspectives. Upon learning about my approach other colleagues shared that they started doing the same thing increasing transparency and building trust among colleagues.

While the initial experience of making myself vulnerable through the 360 feedback process was challenging for both me and new for the organization, obtaining feedback from three dozen colleagues at that point in my career was invaluable and helpful. Through the process I realized there were lots of colleagues who recognized my potential, provided supportive feedback, and wanted me to succeed. Many highlighted several positive traits including my character, integrity, work effort, along with the ability to create and sell a vision and a desire to never be satisfied with the status quo. And as I kept reading, I came across a comment that began with, "Brian is a good man . . ."

(Note to reader: The story continues in the second half of the book on the following page.)

PERSPECTIVES   WHEREFROM   GRANDPARENT   TEAM
UNDERSTAND   BUSINESS EXECUTIVE   LOCKER ROOM
TOGETHER   HELP OTHERS   HOBBIES   EMPOWERING
SOLVE MORE PROBLEMS THAN YOU CAUSE   IMPROVE
COMMUNICATION   CANDID   THINK DIFFERENTLY
TOWARDS THE FUTURE   BELIEVE   POSITIVE INTENT
INCREASE YOUR KNOWLEDGE   BEST   SELF-AWARE
INTEGRITY   CLARITY
RELATIONSHIPS   GROWTH MINDSET   GENUINE   HUMBLE
SEPARATE FACTS FROM FAIRY TALES   EXPECTATIONS
TEACHER   FAILURE IS NECESSARY   CONNECT THE DOTS

PART II

MINDSET MATTERS

*Whether you think you can, or you
think you can't—you're right.*
—Henry Ford

As soon as I read those words ("Brian is a good man"), I checked my pulse to make sure I was not dead and then quickly realized I must be doing something right to earn that compliment.

As I have shared this story over the years, many people reflect and share with me something one of their elder relatives said to them and how it impacted the way they choose to live.

These stories are mostly positive, but occasionally they have created scars or psychological trauma that has stuck with these people for decades. This made me realize the impact our words and attitudes can have on others and the need for me to try to be the best human I can be.

Over time, an overriding theme emerged for me. This led me to create a daily goal to – 'Solve more problems than I cause.' Let's be clear: I am far from perfect in this regard, but overall, my daily scorecard typically has more tick marks in the solutions column than the problems column. Additionally, I take great pride and satisfaction in solving problems and helping others achieve their goals. Doing this is a win-win, but that does not mean it is easy. In fact, if you avoid challenging situations and don't push hard enough to take some calculated chances and have some failures (aka learning experiences), you will never grow. The trick is to find the balance. We all have challenging days at work or at home, but with practice I believe almost everyone (yes, that means you too) can take the "half empty" and make it "half full."

A daily goal: 'Solve more problems than I cause.'

I share this daily goal regularly and freely with many people I encounter, and almost everyone who hears it starts to chuckle. After digesting what I said, many also reply that it is a pretty good goal. I know it sounds funny, but just think if everyone had that mentality that they could make their half-empty glass half full. The world would be a much safer and better place where almost everyone would avoid the front page of their local paper.

To me these six simple words—*solve more problems than I cause*—inspire me each day to be a better parent, husband, boss, colleague, friend, and coach. They are the basis of my Everyday Leadership. Maybe you have your own daily goal, or maybe you like my six words and want to try to make them your goal. If so, the following chapters share some ideas and techniques that work for me. I don't expect that all of them will work for you, but if you apply the concepts to your own life, I am confident you will have more pluses than minuses, and the people around you will feel more positive as well, allowing you to continue further on your journey toward Everyday Leadership.

CHAPTER 10

(A POSITIVE) ATTITUDE IS FREE

Ability is what you're capable of doing.
Motivation determines what you do. Attitude
determines how well you do it.
—Lou Holtz

Some of the most impactful leadership nuggets can come from places you least expect. For example, one morning when I was exercising in my home gym, I was flipping through the stations and pushing the channel button. As I scrolled from ESPN (commercial) to ESPN2 (commercial) to Sports South (commercial) to the Golf Channel (commercial), and finally to MTV, I found an interesting program. MTV was airing an episode of *Austin City Limits* (*ACL*). If you don't know much about *ACL*, it is a weekly PBS television show of music performances. It started in 1974 and is the longest-running music program in television history.[13]

---

13 https://acltv.com/history-of-acl/

ACL features music from all genres. I happened to see an advertisement for an upcoming episode featuring an artist named Ryan Adams. The episode aired back in 2014, well before Adams's "reimagination" of Taylor Swift's *1989* album and while he was still married to Mandy Moore, for which he may be best known. (See chapter 12 for more about their strained relationship.)

I wanted to record and watch the episode, as I really enjoy Adams's song "New York, New York." I thought it would be great to see him perform it live, albeit on recorded television. Eventually, I watched the televised portion of his 2014 performance, and sadly (at least for me) it focused on Adams's latest album and didn't include this hit from earlier in the century. As the musical portion of the show ended, Adams gave a brief commentary. He started off by saying, "The way I try to look at things is…in the last five years of my life I really learned a lot about attitude."

He recounted a story about advice he received from a friend when he was "really tired" from the production and promotion of a past record. He explained to his friend, "Man, I gotta get up and do three interviews today. I have to go do this performance on the BBC and then I have to go do a show."

Then he recounted that his friend responded, "Actually, the way you start that sentence is 'I get to.'" This, according to Adams, was "unbelievable advice" that he wouldn't soon forget. He went on to say, "I get to get up and do this today. I don't know how it's going to be, but I'm going to have an amazing time doing it… I get to do this." There it was—a profound nugget on attitude at the end of an *Austin City Limits* episode. I cannot tell you how many times this insight has changed my day and changed the days of others.

Long before seeing this episode, I got on the elevator at work one morning at a very stressful point in my career. While riding to my floor, I spoke with someone who worked for a different company. She asked how my day was going. "So far so good," I responded sarcastically. "I haven't killed anyone yet." The door opened just as I finished my cynical response. As I started to exit, she said, "I hope that doesn't change." Then the door closed behind me. I paused for a moment and thought about what just occurred. I regularly reflect on how that comment made her feel and how I potentially impacted her day...probably negatively. I don't ever remember seeing that person again, but the only thing she will remember me by was that one snarky comment.

I thought, 'Is that how I want to be thought of or remembered? Is that who I am?'

People who really know me know that's not who I am. But because of this interaction, that is who I will always be to this individual. She doesn't know me, but based on her limited experience with me, she probably wouldn't want to know me any better—she's already seen enough.

Several years later, Paul Aldo (who you will meet later), an executive coach, told me I need to completely remove sarcasm from my communications. Initially, I challenged him on this. I believed I used it to connect with people.

But he shared that too often others view sarcasm as cynicism. Leaders are not successful in the long run if they are cynical. That practice undermines your credibility. Intellectually, I know credibility is paramount to effective Everyday Leadership. Paul was spot-on, but I found it hard to keep my sarcastic comments to myself. Every once in a while, one would slip out.

Just like the other principles of Everyday Leadership discussed in this book, avoiding sarcasm takes practice. But it finally resonated one day when a very intelligent, quick-witted colleague made a sarcastic comment in a meeting and afterward someone said to me, "He's so

---

'Is that how I want to be thought of or remembered? Is that who I am?'

---

cynical."

To help my "sarcastic and cynical colleague," I sought him out and shared my executive coach's feedback and the comment from our colleague. To my surprise, he said, "I'm not changing. That's who I am." Great guy. Full of integrity. High IQ. Fun to be around. But he wouldn't accept the premise that his attitude was getting in his own way.

So, if attitude matters, how do you change it? For me, every day is "Happy!" I enter the building and greet people with "Happy _____-day!" I started doing this in the early 2000s. Every Monday morning during my consulting career, I would walk into the team room and say, "Happy Monday!" This was after getting up when it was still dark to catch an early flight, but it positively impacted the team with which I was working. It became something people looked forward to, and when I took on a leadership role, every morning as I entered the cubicles, I'd address a farm of team members with "Happy (whatever day of the week it was)." I used the phrase on early morning conference calls, and it became synonymous with me, so much so that I didn't even have to say my name because everyone knew it was my "call sign." When I left my job years later, more than a dozen people told me how much they were going to miss my "Happy _____!" greeting every morning. To lighten some of the day's challenges, that positive expression is especially beneficial at the start of difficult meetings or conversations.

Another way to create positivity is to change the conversation. You can end your weekly team meeting with a "Question of the Week," such as "What is your favorite movie? Color? Song? Broadway musical?" During big sporting events, it might be a question like "Who's going to win the World Series? NCAA football playoffs? March Madness? Super Bowl?" As people answer each of these questions, it allows you to learn about the members of your team. More importantly, they get to learn about you and each other.

Having a lunch meeting also changes the conversation, especially if it is a buffet. I also used to bring in lunch for my direct report meetings regularly. It started out of necessity for a meeting one day, and I observed that the team naturally spent time talking about something other than work. They did it while waiting for food and when they then sat back down at the table. Again, I observed them making positive connections that enhanced relationships.

So, what are you going to do to ensure you have and are conveying a positive attitude? It is quite easy to revert to negativity and even display a "poor me" approach when you are faced with adversity or challenges. But that is when you and your team need your positive attitude the most. It can be as simple as a two-word phrase — "get to" or "Happy Monday!" Even if you don't fully believe it, try it on for size. You will find that your attitude will brighten the attitudes of those around you. As you start to see more positive responses to your energy, you will find an almost domino-like impact. And it all started with your initial step. Positivity begets positivity. Remember that water seeks its own level. Knowing that, decide on one or two things you can do each day, week, or month to uplift your team's mentality and attitude. These things can be as small as a catchy greeting, a team lunch, a half-day team-building session once a month, or a reward for the team member who demonstrates the highest team morale.

It is up to you to set the pace and the tone for those you lead: your team, family, students, athletes, or colleagues. If you are negative, they will feel that negativity is acceptable. They may even think it is appropriate for them to return the favor. That is when you set yourself and your stakeholders up for disaster. Funnily enough, most leaders start to look around, wondering exactly why their team maintains such a negative attitude, and the same thing applies to coaches and their athletes as well as parents and their kids. If they just looked in the mirror, half the time they'd find their answer. How could I expect the people I'm leading to be positive if I wasn't positive myself? It was hypocritical at the least but catastrophic at the worst.

As a leader, your attitude is free. It doesn't cost anything to have a positive one. But it is in fact priceless. The cost of having a negative attitude is also incalculable in a negative way, or shall we say, "worthless." Your attitude is as important as, if not more important than, just about anything else you carry with you each day—not just for you but for everyone you meet.

So even on the most difficult days, if you are a leader, remember how fortunate you are to "get to" be in the role, "get to" lead people, "get to" make a difference, "get to" impact others' lives, "get to" say "Happy Monday" and start everyone's week off in a positive way, and "get to" read this book and improve your practice of Everyday Leadership.

CHAPTER 11

START EVERY DAY WITH A WIN

You've got to get up every morning with determination
if you're going to go to bed with satisfaction.
—George Horace Lorimer

If you are a sports fan or have ever played sports, you have likely experienced momentum. This isn't momentum as scientists define it, but a situation where one aspect of the game goes your way, which is followed by something else going your way. It begins what can only be described as a chain reaction, and the next thing you know victory is yours for the taking. But momentum can also go the other way. I am a lifelong suffering Atlanta sports fan, and we have seen our share of momentum go against us, whether it was the 1988 Hawks-Celtics series, infield fly rules for a ball that landed thirty feet in the outfield, the disastrous first inning in game five of the 2019 National League Division Series, or the remarkable implosion of the Atlanta Falcons in Super Bowl LI. Trust me, I know the pain of momentum shifts. But momentum can also be extremely positive as witnessed by the Atlanta Braves 2021 World Series championship run. When the season was two-thirds complete, the team had lost more games than it had won, but then the team won 16 of the next 18 games in early to mid-August and then finished the season in late September and October winning 12 of its last 14 games… momentum that led them to winning the World Series.

Momentum is powerful and you need positive momentum to be an effective Everyday Leader. In fact, you are responsible for generating it. It must start somewhere. I believe it starts in the morning. In a commencement speech to his alma mater, the University of Texas, Admiral William H. McRaven offered ten lessons he learned from basic SEAL training. He did so to provide perspective and help the new graduates achieve the University of Texas slogan: "What starts here changes the world." "Make your bed" was the first lesson he shared, which became the title of his bestselling book.

Admiral McRaven said the following:

"Every morning in basic SEAL training, my instructors, who at the time were all Vietnam veterans, would show up in my barracks room and the first thing they'd do was inspect was my bed. If you did it right, the corners would be square, the covers would be pulled tight, the pillow centered just under the headboard and the extra blanket folded neatly at the foot of the rack.

It was a simple task—mundane at best. But every morning we were required to make our bed to perfection. It seemed a little ridiculous at the time, particularly in light of the fact that we were aspiring to be real warriors, tough battle-hardened SEALs, but the wisdom of this simple act has been proven to me many times over.

If you make your bed every morning, you will have accomplished the first task of the day. It will give you a small sense of pride, and it will encourage you to do another task and another and another. And by the end of the day, that one task completed will have turned into many tasks completed. Making your bed will also reinforce the fact that little things in life matter. If you can't do the little things right, you will never do the big things right.

And, if by chance you have a miserable day, you will come home to a bed that is made—that you made—and a made bed gives you encouragement that tomorrow will be better."[14]

Admiral McRaven went on to share stories and lessons about teamwork, judgment, strength, attitude, resiliency, determination, character, risk, humility, and being your best. While I would like to recognize him for sharing his lessons and thank him for his service to the United States, I would be somewhat scared to tell the admiral (and more scared to tell my mom) that I don't make my

---

14 https://news.utexas.edu/2014/05/16/mcraven-urges-graduates-to-find-courage-to-change-the-world/

bed. But I do subscribe to the admiral's idea that starting the day with an accomplishment is important.

My morning accomplishment is typically exercise. I don't drink coffee, but exercise literally and metaphorically gets my blood flowing. It gives me a sense of accomplishment, relieves stress, and improves my day-to-day mental and physical health. I am typically much more pleasant after I exercise. As the admiral implies, 'Even if I had a bad day, I knew I took care of myself by exercising.'

It is important to start your day in a positive way. It is crucial for you and those around you. I remember driving my son to elementary school one morning. We had a misunderstanding about something so silly I can't even remember the topic. But I remember him crying in the car and being extremely concerned that our interaction was going to ruin the day for him as well as the other students and teachers with whom he would interact. After he got out of the car, I immediately emailed the teacher before I left the school parking lot. I wanted to make sure she checked in with him to help repair the damage. That morning I failed as an Everyday Leader, but I did what I could to fill in the divot I created and engaged others to help and create a win for my son, which they did.

You may not be a morning person but remember that your family and your team senses and feeds off your energy. If you don't have it going for you, then they won't have it going for you or themselves. Organizations, teams, and families take on the characteristics of their leader. These actions create habits; habits create traditions; traditions create culture.

Despite what people post on social media, every day is not sunshine and roses. In fact, many days you are literally or figuratively dealing with poop. But as a leader and someone aspiring to practice Everyday Leadership, you must be positive. Nothing helps positivity and creates a foundation for momentum more than a victory first thing in the morning.

Organizations, teams, and families take on the characteristics of their leader.

In chapter 10: "Attitude Is Free," I shared my morning greeting: "Happy _____!" This expression helped set the tone for the team. A daily huddle is another tool I used at work. Every morning at 8:15 a.m., my direct reports and I spoke on the phone for fifteen minutes, each of us sharing the most important thing that happened yesterday and the most important thing for that day. Sometimes people shared two or three items while occasionally someone took a pass and shared nothing. The goal was to improve communication and share information. But more often than not, the call created positive energy. Many of my direct reports implemented daily huddles with their teams as well, building momentum that cascaded through the organization.

Another idea is the Level 10 meeting structure, which starts off each meeting with each member of the team sharing a personal accomplishment and a professional accomplishment. As one of my colleagues calls it, "Good-Good." This sets a positive tone for the meeting, gives people an opportunity to share, and lets others learn what is going on in teammates' lives at home and at work. This enhances what we know about each other, strengthening relationships and building trust.

Whether it is making your bed, exercising, practicing yoga or meditation, reading the paper, doing the crossword, greeting everyone with a "Happy _____!, implementing a daily huddle, or planning your day, you need to find your morning win. This is not an act or shtick. It must be authentic, real, and genuine to help you effectively practice Everyday Leadership.

People feed off others' energy. When you are positive that energy can spread, but when you are stressed and worried, that energy can spread as well. So stay positive. The best way to be positive is to have a victory to create your own momentum...every morning.

PERSPECTIVES   WHEREFROM   GRANDPARENT   TEAM
UNDERSTAND   BUSINESS EXECUTIVE   LOCKER ROOM
TOGETHER   HELP OTHERS   HOBBIES   EMPOWERING
SOLVE MORE PROBLEMS THAN YOU CAUSE   IMPROVE
COMMUNICATION   CANDID   THINK DIFFERENTLY
TOWARDS THE FUTURE   BELIEVE   POSITIVE INTENT
INCREASE YOUR KNOWLEDGE   BEST   SELF-AWARE
INTEGRITY   WORK   AND   CLARITY
RELATIONSHIPS   GROWTH MINDSET   GENUINE   HUMBLE
SEPARATE FACTS FROM FAIRY TALES   EXPECTATIONS
TEACHER   FAILURE IS NECESSARY   CONNECT THE DOTS

CHAPTER 12

GRAY MATTERS

If you do what's easy, your life will be hard. However,
if you do what's hard, your life will be easy.
—Les Brown

In chapter 10: "Attitude Is Free," I mentioned how I received insights on attitude from an episode of *Austin City Limits* that featured Moore's ex-husband, Ryan Adams. While I was researching this book, approximately five years after the *Austin City Limits* concert, the *New York Times* published an article about Adams. In fact, it was more like an exposé, bringing to light some accusations and descriptions of psychological abuse and sexual misconduct toward women.

To convey the importance of attitude, I obviously felt compelled to share the story. More importantly, I wanted to shed light on the advice his friend offered when suggesting that changing one letter in the phrase ("got to" → "get to") can change your view and how others perceive you. While Adams's attorney clearly disputes the allegations, it was extremely disturbing to read them. But it made me think twice about using the insight Adams shared from his friend. I don't know what happened and am not an advocate for Adams, but I do believe in transparency.

Some might wonder whether I would have included this story if Adams had been indicted or convicted of a crime. For the record and to save the pundits some time, my answer is that it would depend on the crime. But this example shows the important fact that very few things in this world are "all or nothing" or "black and white." Your challenge is to focus on the letters "m" and "e" to expand your thinking from "or" to "more." While I have known a number of people who have "all or nothing" behaviors, attitudes, and approaches to things, I did not know (until researching this chapter) that scholars classify this type of thinking as a "cognitive distortion" or "an automatic way of repeatedly inter-preting a situation that causes us to not consider other ways of thinking about it."[15] It makes sense that there is a classification for it, because we classify everything these days, but it also makes sense because people with an "all or nothing" mentality are very difficult to work with and be around.

People take these one-sided opinions and then create their own team or army to defeat whatever person has made them upset that day. These "destroyers" create their own game with their own rules and their own definition of victory. While many injustices and wrongs need to be righted, some people with extreme positions take the

---

15 http://cogbtherapy.com/cbt-blog/cognitive-distortions-all-or-nothing-thinking

easy way out, by creating lines of good versus evil with no nuance or intention of sustained improvement, just tactical wins by bringing others down.

It is easy to tear things down. It is easy to create division. It is easy to make people look stupid. It is easy to find something someone said or did once in their life, label them, and then "throw the baby out with the bath water." It is easy to be the vigilante. It is easy to keep doing what you are doing. It is easy to blame. It is easy

---

Very few things in this world are "all or nothing" or "black and white." Your challenge is to focus on the letters "m" and "e" to expand your thinking from "or" to "more."

---

to create a conspiracy. It is easy to inflame. It is easy to hurt. It is easy to highlight others' shortcomings. It is easy to tell people what they want to hear.

Instead I challenge you as an Everyday Leader to go beyond the easy . . .

Everyday Leaders do not create headlines; they create progress.

Everyday Leaders do not get their fix; they actually fix.

Everyday Leaders do not seek to make people look stupid; they educate, inform, and build relationships.

Everyday Leaders do not "throw the baby out with the bath water"; they nurture, support, and help people grow.

Everyday Leaders do not take justice into their own hands or create a court of public opinion; they seek changes in the laws and societal norms to improve humanity.

Everyday Leaders do not tear things down; they build things up.

Everyday Leaders do not divide; they bring together and then multiply.

Everyday Leaders do not look for the outlier moments of what people say and do; they look at the whole body of work.

Everyday Leaders do not maintain; they grow.

Everyday Leaders do not blame; they seek to improve.

Everyday Leaders do not focus on conspiracies; they focus on understanding.

Everyday Leaders do not inflame; they heal.

Everyday Leaders do not hurt; they help.

Everyday Leaders do not focus on others' inadequacies; they focus on their own.

Everyday Leaders do not tell people what they want to hear; they tell them the truth or what they need to hear.

Being an Everyday Leader requires courage and strength. You have to sort through the "black and white" and "all or nothing" opinions and use your own gray matter to successfully thrive in the gray.

PERSPECTIVES   WHEREFROM   GRANDPARENT   TEAM
UNDERSTAND   BUSINESS EXECUTIVE   LOCKER ROOM
TOGETHER   HELP OTHERS   HOBBIES   EMPOWERING
SOLVE MORE PROBLEMS THAN YOU CAUSE   IMPROVE
COMMUNICATION   CANDID   THINK DIFFERENTLY
TOWARDS THE FUTURE   BELIEVE   POSITIVE INTENT
INCREASE YOUR KNOWLEDGE   BEST   SELF-AWARE
INTEGRITY   CLARITY
RELATIONSHIPS   GROWTH MINDSET   GENUINE   HUMBLE
SEPARATE FACT   EXPECTATIONS
TEACHER   FAILURE IS NECESSARY   CONNECT THE DOTS

CHAPTER 13

OVERCOME YOUR WEAKNESSES

You are strong when you know your weaknesses.
You are beautiful when you appreciate your flaws.
You are wise when you learn from your mistakes.
—Author unknown

You probably have not heard of Michael Brody-Waite. He is the author of *Great Leaders Live Like Drug Addicts*. This title is similar to his TEDx talk "Great Leaders Do What Drug Addicts Do." Michael starts the talk by informing the audience that he is an addict. I encourage you to watch it and listen as he explains the three survival skills he learned in rehabilitation:

1. Practicing rigorous authenticity
2. Surrendering the outcome
3. Doing uncomfortable work

He learned he would relapse and probably be dead if he did not operate with authenticity, do the correct thing regardless of the outcome, and push himself out of his comfort zone. His lesson goes beyond using this approach to stay sober; he shares that these same tools allowed him to reach his dream of becoming a CEO. He shares how afraid he was at various points to be authentic.

In his TEDx talk, he describes how these principles were integrated into his company's interviewing process, where he always asked, "What is your greatest weakness?" Most people know that someone might ask them this question, and they find a weakness that is a strength. Like "I am an overachiever," or "I work too hard," or "I struggle with work life-balance," or "I'm a perfectionist who focuses on the details." Those are great answers, but they are masks that attempt to hide the real weakness. Knowing your weaknesses is also important because you need to know when to get help.

Knowing when and where you need help is a sign of self-awareness, not a sign of weakness. If you are self-aware, you can surround yourself with people who think differently and/or have different skill sets. You have to hire people who are better and more equipped to do their job than you are. If at any point you believe you can do any of your direct reports' jobs better than they can, then you are both in the wrong job.

You will always be questioning their decisions if you believe this, taking on work they should be doing, and not giving them the opportunity to learn, grow, develop and quite possibly do the job better than the way you think it should be done. And if you are constantly concerned about how they are doing their job, then you as a leader won't be able to do your own job well.

In my first executive role, I "walked this talk" by hiring leaders who were much better and smarter than me for their roles. Fortunately for me, it is not hard to do that. These leaders complemented my weaknesses and also challenged me and each other to be better. This was a diverse group of leaders with different backgrounds and viewpoints. At one point, I had nine direct reports, eight of whom were either female or minority. Five were married. Two had kids very early in life. Three did not have children. One was a former division one college athlete. One had served in the military. One was

---

Knowing your weaknesses is also important because you need to know when to get help.

---

a vegan. Two had grandkids. One loved dogs. Two had children with special needs. One grew up on a farm. A different one owned and lived on a farm. One had four kids (at last count) that are twenty-five years apart in age from oldest to youngest. Two had extensive careers in consulting. Three more dabbled in consulting. One lived an hour north of the office. One lived an hour south. One lived in Athens, Georgia. One commuted from South Carolina. One is a demo chef for Big Green Egg. One is writing a cookbook. One rarely cooked. Two were very strong project managers. Five were very strong operators.

In my opinion, this was the most diverse leadership team in any business unit in the company. Their different experiences and backgrounds provided insights and perspectives I could never have. Way more often than not, this helped tremendously as we made decisions.

We all had our individual weaknesses. One of mine is that I am not the most effective leader of frontline or hourly staff. My background in consulting put me into a position where I learned how to lead salaried team members, but I had very limited experience directly leading hourly team members. To be clear, I have tremendous

---

If at any point you believe you can do any of your direct reports' jobs better than they can, then you are both in the wrong job.

---

respect and admiration for frontline team members and supervisors. They are critical to the success of every organization's mission. That said, middle and frontline leaders must spend more time than I would prefer on policy-related items like attendance and dress code issues. So when I was leading a team of 1,500 members, 90% of which were hourly, I hired very strong operators who had experience with and enjoyed developing, coaching, and leading our frontline team members.

Another of my weaknesses is that I don't take time to celebrate. When I complete a milestone, project, or goal, I immediately look to find the next hill to climb. I learned that unfortunately most of my direct reports also shared that weakness. As a result, we had to be very intentional about collecting, communicating, and celebrating our accomplishments. To help, we had a couple of people who put together newsletters for our team and leadership. In addition, I sent out monthly updates. For several years, I went to every department at least once a year to do a town hall. The executive directors did the same. As we grew, we empowered the directors to celebrate and allocated $50 per team member as part of their annual budget for discretionary spending.

That said, historically I have taken too much personal satisfaction from work. While I am still far from perfect in this regard, I am much better than I was during the first ten years of my career. (This is also closely tied to the time my first child was born.) In summary, during the early portion of my career, my day at work defined the quality of my entire day. Maybe that happened because I served in a role where there was always more work than time or people to do it or maybe it happened because that's just who I am. Nevertheless, it was extremely unhealthy, and it's something that I still have to constantly be mindful of and monitor.

Another one (well, actually two) of my weaknesses is that I am not a politician and do not have a poker face. I call it like I see it, and I wear my emotions on my sleeve. I always thought that if I was invited to a meeting, I was supposed to speak up; but I eventually learned that certain cultures expect some people to be seen but not heard.

Learning such things on the fly is part of maturing, but I needed help as I entered a new jungle (after taking an executive role). As a result, I sought out an internal mentor. While there were several talented and experienced executives, my boss and I felt that no one really fit the bill, as my style was different from everyone else's. I was so different that I thought I was "broken." So I asked my boss (the CFO of the company) for an executive coach because I felt I needed an outside perspective to help me become successful in this new role.

The organization found a gentleman, Paul Aldo, who had several years of experience in consulting and industry. He created his own company, Executive Presence, to help people become better executives. I was excited to start. I was expecting a few changes that were going to make me a successful executive. During the process, we had regular meetings and I read Paul's great book *Understanding Executive Presence*. I engaged in a second 360 feedback that included more than thirty-five people and Paul interviewed numerous peers, executives, and direct reports with whom I worked. I also completed the DiSC Assessment which identifies one's operating style through four profiles: (D)ominance, (i)nfluence, (S)teadiness and (C)onscientiousness.[16]

After reviewing everything, he was ready to give me his feedback and ideas for improvement. I was nervous but also extremely excited to receive this revolutionary feedback. In my office, we shared updates about what

---

16 https://www.discprofile.com/what-is-disc/

had been going on personally and professionally—all of which was the undercard to the big reveal.

So he said, "Brian, after reviewing everything, I know you were concerned that you were 'broken' and needed to be fixed, and that is definitely not the case." I now felt somewhat relieved, but I still wanted to know what I needed to do.

He went on to highlight my strengths and provided accolades. He then said, "There are some tiny tweaks you can make that I believe will help you be a lot more effective."

So again, I was ready for the curtain to rise, and when it did, he said, "I want you to focus on walking slower."

A few paragraphs ago, I shared that I don't have a poker face. I had a strange look on mine, along with the empty bubble above my head, and eventually my mouth said, "Uhhhh…Did you say to walk slower?"

He said, with a big smile, "Yes. That is what you should focus on."

I sat there dumbfounded as I tried to figure out what to say or do next. After several seconds of awkward silence, I said, "Okay. Is there anything else?"

Paul responded as he shook his head, "No." Then we ended our meeting and found a date for our next meeting a couple of weeks out.

Paul left, and I remained in disbelief, but I tried to digest and implement his recommendation. At first, I did not notice a difference, but after a couple of days of walking slower, I found myself eating slower, talking slower, responding slower. In fact, everything slowed down.

By slowing down, I was more able to tune in to the moment. I was more attentive and found that I was a better active listener at home and work. Some would call this mindfulness or at least being on a path toward mindfulness. Regardless of what you call it, it was helpful. Actually, it was amazing how much it helped my mindset, my relationships, my focus, my ability to stay calm (most of the time), and my executive presence.

Am I now perfect? Absolutely not. I communicated this opportunity publicly to many people, especially my diverse team of direct reports. Because I openly shared this opportunity and empowered everyone in my entire division, sometimes frontline team members who saw me walking briskly by their cubicles offered a "slow down" or a "you're moving pretty quickly."

It would be great if there was a single answer or path, like a superpower, that each of us could use to overcome our weaknesses. But just like superheroes, who also have many strengths, each of us has our own unique weaknesses. It could be something obvious like kryptonite to Superman, but it could also be something that you cannot see, like the psychological trauma Batman experienced. Regardless of your weakness, it is probably keeping you from being your best self. So whether Michael Brody-Waite's revolutionary approach to improvement or my tweaks seem more in line with what you need, I encourage you to figure out what you need. I urge you to find the resources that can complement you and support you on your journey to overcome your weaknesses and become a better Everyday Leader.

CHAPTER 14

FAILURE IS NECESSARY

Fail big. You will fail at some point in your life. Accept it. You will lose. You will embarrass yourself. You will suck at something. There's no doubt about it.
—Denzel Washington

So often people say, "Failure is not an option." In reality, targeted and calculated failure is necessary for growth and improvement in both people and organizations. In fact, this book is full of stories of my failures and learning experiences. I describe them to provide you insights and an opportunity to learn through another person's experiences and mistakes instead of experiencing the pain directly yourself.

Trevor Ragan focuses on researching, writing, and teaching others about "how 'learning' works and how we can do it better." Trevor starts his TEDx talk[17] on the topic by saying: "To summarize what I have discovered on that journey, we have to start where everybody starts when they talk about learning. And that's by talking about tigers."

---

17 https://trainugly.com/portfolio/tedx-talks/

Tigers? Did he say tigers? Not exactly the first thing that comes to mind when you think about learning. He goes on to compare two tigers: one that lives in a zoo and another that lives in the jungle. The zoo tiger has every meal delivered, along with water, shelter, and safety, while jungle tigers must figure out how to find water and food while protecting themselves from other predators. Although these two types of tigers are born with basically the same DNA, as long as the zoo tiger stays in the zoo, it will never grow and develop like the jungle tiger, because it is not in an environment where it needs to learn and develop the skills required for survival. The zoo tiger does not experience the daily issues or changes or environmental factors that would allow it to develop and use its innate skills and abilities.

When given the choice, most people choose to be the zoo tiger. It has a comfortable life. You can live a sustained life and make the best of the environment in many ways without realizing that another option exists. I have been the zoo tiger for most of my life. For various reasons, I have chosen stability and managed or sustained growth. Early in my career, I had several opportunities to jump to a different consulting firm where I could have made 20% to 30% more money. Numerous "once-in-a-lifetime career opportunities" came my way, many of which would have involved moving my family to different parts of the country. But I, along with my wife, have chosen to balance my career growth and aspirations with our desire to keep my family in my hometown of Atlanta so our kids are near my parents and other close family members. That said, I have grown and built my career. I was fortunate to have executives and mentors who provided opportunities throughout the first twenty years of my career including most recently during my 12-year tenure at a prominent health care system, a beacon of quality for health care in the southeastern United States.

While I could have remained a zoo tiger in that organization, I decided to parachute into the jungle. The jungle is scary. The jungle has lots of unknowns. But the jungle also has lots of opportunity. The jungle can enhance existing relationships and build new ones. In fact, I have been humbled and flattered by all the support colleagues provided when I began this journey. Going into the jungle has provided me the space and opportunity to try new things—things that I don't do well, was scared to do, or that made me vulnerable: writing this book, having consulting clients, and asking for help from others. Jungle, jungle, jungle. These are things I could not have done if I had stayed in the zoo.

Early on in this journey, I sought the assistance of a new executive coach, Jeanette Matern. After I got through the emotional part of jumping out of the organizational plane and realizing I was in the jungle, she asked me, "What does the top of your mountain look like?" I responded, "I want to write my book and do speaking." She then asked, "What other mountains are in your range?" To be clear, she was not trying to deter me; this was a reality check to see how far into the jungle I was willing to go. There were and still are many mountains in my range where I can be helicoptered in as an executive. Writing a book and speaking were not just about climbing a mountain. It was a mountain I would have to build and climb. Given my vast knowledge, skills, abilities, experience, and network within health care finance and nonprofit companies, it definitely made more sense to be helicoptered in, get established, and keep the dream of the book on the back burner.

Covid-19 came along and changed those plans. I could have easily sulked and just waited for things to open back up, but instead I decided to build and climb the book mountain. I took the lead on the things that I don't do well (writing, marketing, self-promotion), was scared to do (go out on my own), and made me vulnerable (putting myself out there for everyone to read and critique as well as asking for help).

Throughout my career, I have always shared with my team and clients the importance of pushing for improvements. I have urged them to make calculated gambles to go even further and "push the envelope." Implementing and achieving change is hard. Businesspeople, especially top performers, do not want to fail, so I had to communicate that it is okay to fail. I came up with the mantra, 'If you're not failing at something, you're not trying hard enough.' While expecting my team to follow this principle, I was not practicing what I was preaching. While I am sure my family and coworkers might compile a scroll full of examples, I could not think of the last time I really failed.

Again, I was a zoo tiger.

I had to enter the jungle. As I once heard from Steve Olson, a professor of entrepreneurship and innovation, in an executive leadership course, "You can't export what you don't produce."

When I communicate that "failing is necessary," I am not trying to put the team or organization in a position where there could be a massive or catastrophic failure. Instead, I am calling for targeted, needle-moving efforts that go outside the box to improve the business and provide opportunities for the team. That said, I realize that more often than not these efforts and initiatives pay off in multiple ways. The business has better results (increased revenue and productivity along with decreased turnover), and the team members and leaders feel tremendous pride

---

'If you're not failing at something, you're not trying hard enough.'

---

when they accomplish something that seemed beyond their capabilities. And the shared learning experience brings the team closer together and builds trust even when something does not work.

These same philosophies apply on the home front. It makes perfect sense when you look at how babies, toddlers, and kids learn. My daughter, who is three years-old at the time of this writing (and four years-old at the time of publishing), learns through failure. Whether it is from toys like the shape sorter or life skills like learning to drink from a cup, using a utensil, and using the restroom, she learns through failure.

As I shared earlier in the book, my son, who is currently thirteen, loves sports. As a sports fan myself, this is great for me. As they say, "The apple doesn't fall far from the tree." He loves both watching and playing sports.

Occasionally, he competes in tennis tournaments. Tennis is a unique sport in that you cannot communicate with or coach the participants during their competition. You are not even supposed to cheer or recognize the opponent for a great shot. It is a jungle.

As a result, these tournaments are stressful for kids. They are competing on their own, trying to figure everything out while calling their own lines and keeping score. It is a lot for these kids to handle. A jungle every time.

Tennis has another jungle in addition to being out there on the court all alone and managing various aspects of play. It is a sport filled with failure. Even the best players—Nadal, Federer, McEnroe, and Ashe lose (or lost) around 20% of their matches.[18]

Just think—half the players go home from every professional tournament not winning a single match because they lost in the first round. A July 2018 *New York Times* article[19] provides amazing statistics:

> According to data provided by ATPWorldTour. com, 567 men have played at least 200 matches in its 45-year history, and only 277 of them have a

---

18 https://www.atptour.com/en/performance-zone/win-loss-index/career/all/all/ as of June 2020
19 https://www.nytimes.com/2018/07/13/sports/tennis/pro-tennis-tour-failure.html

positive win-loss record. According to the WTA Tour, 320 women have played at least 200 matches, and only 169 have a winning record. If you reduce the criteria to 100-plus matches, then only 291 of 819 men have a better than .500 percentage, while on the women's tour, it is 186 of 563.

In summary, for the 1,382 men and women who have played more than 200 matches at the highest levels of tennis, only approximately 34% of them have a winning record.

Julien Benneteau, who is mentioned and quoted in the *New York Times* article, is a prime example. He retired in 2019 with a career singles record of 273–297. His highest ranking was twenty-fifth in the world, but he never won a professional singles tournament. "I have known failure because I lost every week," he said. "Then I have to recover and think positively to be ready for the next week and do this week after week, month after month, year after year, to have a career from 2000 to now." [20] This comes from a guy who had a winning record in doubles, including a Grand Slam win, and who earned over $9.5 million in his tennis career. Strong words. Tough sport.

Although kids' tournaments typically have a consolation bracket, more kids will lose two matches before they win three matches. This is a controlled jungle, a place for them to learn and grow. As a result, a tremendous number of benefits come with playing.

---

20 https://www.nytimes.com/2018/07/13/sports/tennis/pro-tennis-tour-failure.html

First, playing gets and keeps a child physically active and off screens. Second, the unique conditions help develop problem-solving skills. Third, the child has to learn how to deal with failure, and that builds character. Fourth, the child sees how his effort can lead to personal improvement and potentially better performance and outcomes. Fifth, it is a lifelong sport.

Sure, my son wants to win a trophy. (Note that there are no participation trophies in tennis.) But what is important in our home are three things:

1. Good effort
2. Good sportsmanship
3. Good attitude

We are proud when these things happen, regardless of the scoreboard.

In fact, we have an expectation in our home that if our son wins a tournament, he comes home, empties the dishwasher, and plays with his sister. If he loses, he comes home, empties the dishwasher, and plays with his sister.

Ironically, I learned about Trevor Ragan from the United States Tennis Association (USTA). The association is beginning to focus on adding resources to improve the mental capabilities of players in addition to their stroke, strategy, footwork, and other technical tennis skills.

As a parent and someone touting the principles of Everyday Leadership, I am 100% supportive and excited for the USTA to support the mental aspects of the game more directly and assist their stakeholders to learn from the sense of failure the sport creates. As a father, husband, son, mentor, friend, and "regular guy" just trying to practice becoming better at Everyday Leadership, I am excited to have entered the jungle and am already learning from my failures. I expect to learn a lot more as the journey continues.

Think about your roles and your impact on others, the things you want to be known for, and the legacy you want to leave. Are you pushing yourself to grow, learn, and develop, or are you staying in the cage where it is safe? Go produce by demonstrating your willingness to enter the jungle, or you will never be able to export this concept to those you are leading, much less to practice Everyday Leadership. And as Jim Carrey said in a 2014 commencement speech at Maharishi International University, "You can fail at what you don't want, so you might as well take a chance on doing what you love."[21]

As a father, husband, son, mentor, friend, and "regular guy" just trying to practice becoming better at Everyday Leadership, I am excited to have entered the jungle and am already learning from my failures. I expect to learn a lot more as the journey continues.

---

21 https://www.rev.com/blog/transcripts/jim-carrey-commencement-speech-transcript-2014-at-maharishi-university-of-management

CHAPTER 15

TWO KINDS OF THINKING

*Five percent of the people think; ten percent of
the people think they think; and the other eighty-
five percent would rather die than think.*
—Thomas A. Edison

My leadership style is somewhat different from that typical in corporate America. As part of my style, I like to throw out lots of ideas. In fact, I tell colleagues and direct reports that my style is to throw out ten ideas, and it is totally okay if we do the exact opposite of just one of them. While some may think this is my way of being passive aggressive, it is the exact opposite. I simply want to push forward. I aim to get everyone to put aside their preconceived notions and thoughts. I'm trying to create an environment for a growth mindset where people will feel comfortable exploring, coming up with ideas, putting many brains together to gain multiple perspectives, generating discussion, feeding off each other, engaging in the process, and allowing our innate curiosity to blossom. I know, firsthand, this improves the knowledge of stakeholders and creates the best path forward.

To that point, I would like to put forward two types of thinking. The first kind of thinking is the act of generating ideas. For example, you might say "I was thinking that we should have sushi for dinner." The second kind is thinking that you know something or know how to do something. In my case, you would say "I think I am going to make sushi for dinner." The first is an idea. The second is a disaster waiting to happen. To go a step further, people who always "think they know" are very dangerous to be around—almost as dangerous as the people who think they are something they are not.

For me, that might mean I thought I was a sushi chef. Don't get me wrong, I have sat at many sushi bars and watched qualified people (also known as chefs) make sushi. In fact, I have watched hundreds of rolls being made, which is almost as many as I have eaten. I can go to the store and buy all the items you need to make sushi. Or better yet, I could go on Amazon and buy a sushi-making kit (with instructions) for under $30. I can purchase the rice, seaweed, fish, vegetables, sauces, etc., but that does not mean I can successfully make sushi.

It is subtle, but I see it happen every day. People enter a situation thinking they know the problem, know the answer, and how to solve the issue. Maybe that's because they have seen it done before, overestimate their own abilities, see only part of the issue, or do not value the knowledge, skill, and expertise required to execute the task successfully.

What you know coming into a situation, may or may not be at an appropriate level of skill to get you to the finish line. Your knowledge could be outdated, limited, or flat-out incorrect. As leaders, we must go beyond the first insight to really get a full perspective. Is it firsthand knowledge? Secondhand knowledge? Or thirdhand knowledge? Understand your source(s) to know if they were provided by someone with limited knowledge or someone with a specific objective to have you see the information a certain way. In some instances, your pre-

---

People who always "think they know" are very dangerous to be around—almost as dangerous as the people who think they are something they are not.

---

vious knowledge may be outright dangerous or harmful. Heck, I might not know how to keep the raw fish fresh, and thus inadvertently self-induce food poisoning.

When I entered the workforce as a staff consultant at Ernst & Young, I was intimidated by a few people in my starting class. They had come from some of the top schools in the country as undergraduates and MBAs. When I first saw them, I could see they were polished and more "buttoned up." They had confidence, and some (unfortunately) were cocky.

It was clear that many of these folks were smart, but I quickly learned that my effort, resourcefulness, and ability to question and see things differently set me apart from those who might have more raw intelligence. While it might have partly been grit or resilience, I believe the quality that set me apart was something else entirely: *curiosity*.

CHAPTER 16

CURIOSITY

The important thing is not to stop questioning. Curiosity has its own reason for existing. One cannot help but be in awe when he contemplates the mysteries of eternity, of life, of the marvelous structure of reality. It is enough if one tries merely to comprehend a little of this mystery every day.
—Albert Einstein

As we consider the difference between the two types of thinking described in the previous chapter, I would submit that the greatest difference comes from a single character trait: curiosity. Producing and sharing ideas is a form of generating curiosity, while thinking you know the answer is the exact opposite. Researchers have written a great deal about intelligence, but relatively little has been said about curiosity. What has been published, however, is somewhat enlightening. While the text that follows is somewhat different from the most recent story-based chapters, I recognize people learn in different ways. Thus, this information should connect with you (the reader) on different (emotional and intellectual) levels, but it has the same intent of expanding and promoting Everyday Leadership. In addition, it sets the stage for how curiosity has positively impacted my life in the chapters that follow.

In 1899, philosopher and psychologist William James called curiosity "the impulse towards better cognition"—in other words, wanting to improve your understanding of what you do not know.[22]

Thomas Friedman,[23] a three-time Pulitzer Prize winner and a weekly *New York Times* columnist, puts forward a similar theory in his book *The World Is Flat*. Friedman suggests that in today's world, where information is ubiquitous, it is more important to have both curiosity (CQ) and passion (PQ) than intelligence. Friedman states, "Give me the kid with a passion to learn and a curiosity to discover and I will take him or her over the less passionate kid with a huge IQ every day of the week. Curious, passionate kids are self-educators and self-motivators. They will always be able to learn how to learn." Friedman then quotes Doc Searls, who says, "Work matters, but curiosity matters more. Nobody works harder at learning than a curious kid."[24]

In a 2014 *Harvard Business Review* article, Tomas Chamorro-Premuzic[25] wrote:

---

22 C. Kidd and B.Y. Hayden, "The Psychology and Neuroscience of Curiosity," Neuron, 88(3) (2015): 449–460, https://doi.org/10.1016/j.neuron.2015.09.010.

23 https://en.wikipedia.org/wiki/Thomas_Friedman

24 https://www.goodreads.com/work/quotes/711993-the-world-is-flat-a-brief-history-of-the-twenty-first-century

25 Tomas Chamorro-Premuzic is the Chief Talent Scientist at Manpower Group, cofounder of Deeper Signals and Metaprofiling, and professor of business psychology at University College London and Columbia University, https://drtomas.com/about/.

"People with higher CQ are more inquisitive and open to new experiences. They find novelty exciting and are quickly bored with routine. They tend to generate many original ideas and are counter-conformist. It has not been as deeply studied as EQ and IQ, but there's some evidence to suggest it is just as important when it comes to managing complexity in two major ways. First, individuals with higher CQ are generally more tolerant of ambiguity. This nuanced, sophisticated, subtle thinking style defines the very essence of complexity. Second, CQ leads to higher levels of intellectual investment and knowledge acquisition over time, especially in formal domains of education, such as science and art (note: this is of course different from IQ's measurement of raw intellectual horsepower). Knowledge and expertise, much like experience, translate complex situations into familiar ones, so CQ is the ultimate tool to produce simple solutions for complex problems."

These quotes resonate with me, but I recognize that they are also anecdotal. In a 2017 article for *Greater Good Magazine*, "Why Curious People Have Better Relationships," Jill Suttie highlights the findings from a few research studies on curiosity. One of her conclusions: "Studies have found that people who are curious are often viewed in social encounters as more interesting and engaging, and they are more apt to reach out to a wider variety of people. In addition, being curious seems to protect people from negative social experiences, like rejection, which could lead to better connection with others over time."[26]

Adam Bryant, who interviewed more than 525 CEOs for the *New York Times* "Corner Office" column, believes the "X-factor" that explains why people became CEOs "beyond obvious ones like hard work and perseverance" is "applied curiosity."[27]

What is applied curiosity? Bryant describes it as follows:

> "It means trying to understand how things work, and then trying to understand how they can be made to work better. It means being curious about people and their backstories. It means using insights to build deceptively simple frameworks and models in their minds to make sense of their industry—and all the other disruptive forces shaping our world—so they can explain it to others. Then they continue asking questions about those models, and it's those questions that often lead to breakthrough ideas."

Two of the CEOs he quotes are:

- Alan R. Mulally, the former chief executive of Ford Motor Company: "You learn from everybody. I've always just wanted to learn everything, to

---

26 https://greatergood.berkeley.edu/article/item/why_curious_people_have_better_relationships

27 https://www.linkedin.com/pulse/ive-interviewed-hundreds-ceos-all-share-one-habit-mind-adam-bryant/

understand anybody that I was around—why they thought what they did, why they did what they did, what worked for them, what didn't work."

- Michael Dowling, the chief executive of Northwell Health, said that the qualities he looks for in job candidates include relationship skills and a positive attitude, but also a third quality: "Instead of their I.Q., I want to know their C.Q.—their curiosity quotient." He further noted, "To what extent are you focused on figuring out how to improve whatever it is you're going to be doing? Nothing is perfect, so you should always be trying to figure out how to make it better."

In a trilogy of *Harvard Business Review* articles on curiosity, many authors share research and insights about how curiosity is an overlooked attribute and underutilized cultural approach to improve business. In "The Business Case for Curiosity,"[28] Francesca Gino writes there are benefits to curiosity: better decision-making, increased innovation, reduced group conflict, and improved communication and team performance.

In a second article, "From Curious to Competent," leaders from the executive search firm Egon Zehnder share that in their thirty years of evaluating candidates' potential and competence, "you can't have either without curiosity." The authors say that competence is also necessary to make it to the C-suite, and the best way

---

28 https://hbr.org/2018/09/curiosity#the-business-case-for-curiosity

to enhance the competence of the curious is through providing them stretch assignments. They found people with increased competence had "worked for more companies, [have] been exposed to more diverse customers, worked abroad or with colleagues from other cultures, dealt with more business scenarios (start-ups, rapid growth, M&A, integration, downsizing, turnarounds), and managed more people. When curious people are given these experiences, they shine. When they aren't, they either stagnate or jump ship." [29]

The third article in the *Harvard Business Review* series, "The Five Dimensions of Curiosity," focuses on different ways people express curiosity. While the authors found correlations between curiosity and success, just like everything, the two are not necessarily predictors of one another. Although most are positive, some potentially negative behaviors are also associated with curiosity, such as gossip and thrill seeking, which could turn into risk taking activities.[30]

As for enhancing curiosity in your organization, Gino shares five ways:

1. **Hire for curiosity.** Gino writes, "In 2004 an anonymous billboard appeared on Highway 101, in the heart of Silicon Valley, posing this puzzle: "{first 10-digit prime found in consecutive digits

---

29 https://hbr.org/2018/09/from-curious-to-competent?ab=seriesnav-spotlight

30 Todd B. Kashdan, David J. Disabato, Fallon R. Goodman, and Carl Naughton, "The Five Dimensions of Curiosity," *Harvard Business Review*, https://hbr.org/2018/09/the-five-dimensions-of-curiosity?ab=seriesnav-spotlight

of e}.com." The answer, 7427466391.com, led the curious online, where they found another equation to solve. The handful of people who did so were invited to submit a résumé to Google. The company took this unusual approach to finding job candidates because it places a premium on curiosity. (People didn't even need to be engineers!) As Eric Schmidt, Google's CEO from 2001 to 2011, has said, 'We run this company on questions, not answers.'"

Personally, I tell people I like to hire "athletes" into leadership positions. What I mean by that is that I want people who can play multiple positions on the team. Sometimes you need a specialist who has a specific role, but more often than not when it comes to leadership, someone who has demonstrated the ability to play multiple positions typically has proven to have curious tendencies.

2. **Model inquisitiveness.** While "listen" and "silent" have the same letters and are tangentially related, you can't always remain silent if you want to know what is really going on. You have to ask open-ended questions and actively listen to the response. The Greek philosopher Epictetus said we have two ears and one tongue, which means we should listen twice as much as we talk. Gino writes, "That may seem intuitive, but my research shows that we often prefer to talk rather than to listen with curiosity. For instance, when I asked

some 230 high-level leaders in executive education classes what they would do if confronted with an organizational crisis stemming from both financial and cultural issues, most said they would take action: move to stop the financial bleeding and introduce initiatives to refresh the culture. Only a few said they would ask questions rather than simply impose their ideas on others."

3. **Emphasize learning goals.** Gino refers to an interview with Captain Chesley "Sully" Sullenberger, who famously made an emergency landing of a commercial airplane in the Hudson River. She writes, "He described his passion for continuous learning." She adds, "Although commercial flights are almost always routine, every time his plane pushed back from the gate, he would remind himself that he needed to be prepared for the unexpected. What can I learn? he would think. When the unexpected came to pass, on a cold January day in 2009, Sully was able to ask himself what he could do, given the available options, and come up with a creative solution. He successfully fought the tendency to grasp for the most obvious option (landing at the nearest airport). Especially when under pressure, we narrow in on what immediately seems the best course of action. But those who are passionate about continuous learning contemplate a wide range of options and perspectives. As the accident report shows, Sully

carefully considered several alternatives in the 208 seconds between his discovery that the aircraft's engines lacked thrust and his landing of the plane in the Hudson."

This line of thinking is not just for airline pilots. One day when my son was in 3rd or 4th grade, he came home with an activity he completed. It said, "Don't be a Fixed Freddie." After some research, I learned the opposite of a "Fixed Freddie" is someone with a "Growth Mindset." Carol Dweck explains this concept in a 2012 interview[31]:

> "In a fixed mindset, students believe their basic abilities, their intelligence, their talents, are just fixed traits. They have a certain amount and that's that, and then their goal becomes to look smart all the time and never look dumb. In a growth mindset, students understand that their talents and abilities can be developed through effort, good teaching, and persistence. They don't necessarily think everyone's the same or anyone can be Einstein, but they believe everyone can get smarter if they work at it."

4. **Let employees explore and broaden their interests.** As previously mentioned in Chapter 6: "Old MacDonald Had a Farm E-or-I, E-or-I-Oh...Sh★t," giving curious high-potential

---

31 https://onedublin.org/2012/06/19/stanford-universitys-carol-dweck-on-the-growth-mindset-and-education/

employees stretch assignments helps them develop needed competencies. Starting in 2014, as the newly appointed Microsoft CEO, Satya Nadella began changing the company's culture. After a nine-month effort, Kathleen Hogan, Microsoft's Chief Human Resources Officer describes it as "moving from the sense of a bunch of know-it-alls to a bunch of learn-it-alls." Additionally, Hogan describes what they seek in job candidates, "We look for curiosity and learning."[32]

5. **Have "Why?" "What if?" and "How might we?" days.** As an executive in one organization, I conducted a couple of different innovation days to develop strategy, vision, and priorities for my team. I named one of them "Idea Survivor," where I asked all the directors (approximately three dozen people) to bring their top ideas. I grouped them into five interdisciplinary teams, asked them to discuss their ideas with each other, and select one idea to present to their bosses/my direct reports. Two of the teams had similar ideas, and we took those forward, ultimately replacing a longtime vendor with one that had a new, updated solution to increase the accuracy of information and enhance its integration to the main technology system. This reduced the number of errors caused

---

32 https://www.businessinsider.com/microsoft-hr-chief-kathleen-hogan-company-culture-change-satya-nadella-2019-8

by "human middleware," where team members were taking information from one system and then choosing and updating the appropriate field in a different system that was the source of truth. This project decreased the amount of time it took to register patients and improved financial results. But more importantly, it engaged the directors who now knew not only we cared about innovation and what they thought, but we acted on their recommendations.

In summary, to be an effective Everyday Leader, you have to create an environment where your team, family, and followers can be the "curious kid." Unfortunately, we are overwhelmed by inputs, so making and taking

---

In summary, to be an effective Everyday Leader, you have to create an environment where your team, family, and followers can be the "curious kid."

---

time to think, wonder, and dream is important. Yes, everyone has a job to do, and I recognize tasks have to get done, but you need people to "connect the dots" not just "check the box." The only way to get them to connect the dots is to stop reacting and start thinking. As an Everyday Leader, you should demonstrate and create an environment that fosters curiosity. When you do, you will improve stakeholder engagement and light a fire in your team. The result will drive engagement and yield improved productivity, efficiency, and accuracy. At the same time, you will create a culture of continuous improvement in your followers and the processes, because people will bring forward their ideas to enhance performance. Ultimately, they will not just think but *know* they can make a positive impact.

The power of curiosity should not be underestimated. Leverage it to create momentum and growth for yourself, your team, and your organization.

PERSPECTIVES WHEREFROM GRANDPARENT TEAM
UNDERSTAND BUSINESS EXECUTIVE LOCKER ROOM
TOGETHER HELP OTHERS HOBBIES EMPOWERING
SOLVE MORE PROBLEMS THAN YOU CAUSE IMPROVE
COMMUNICATION CANDID THINK DIFFERENTLY
TOWARDS THE FUTURE BELIEVE POSITIVE INTENT
INCREASE YOUR KNOWLEDGE BEST SELF-AWARE
INTEGRITY WORK-LIFE BALANCE AND CLARITY
RELATIONSHIPS GROWTH MINDSET GENUINE HUMBLE
SEPARATE EXPECTATIONS
TEACHER FAILURE IS NECESSARY CONNECT THE DOTS

CHAPTER 17

ONE QUESTION (OR CONVERSATION) CAN CHANGE YOUR LIFE

It's through curiosity and looking at opportunities in new ways that we've always mapped our path.
—Michael Dell

"Will you marry me?" is definitely a life-changing question. So is the discussion of whether you're ready to have kids. (Please know that when you have the conversation, you'll never think that you're really ready). For most people, those are planned questions. But more often than not, the most life-changing moments are not planned.

In Fall 1996, I was a fifth-year senior, one semester away from graduating from the University of Florida (UF). Knowing I would need to enter the "real world" soon, I attended a career expo for the first time. I felt like a deer in headlights, actually a baby deer in headlights. I meandered through the booths of dozens of companies, occasionally stopping to talk with various recruiters and employees who saw me as Bambi and yet were extremely gracious and helpful.

When I was getting ready to leave, I spotted an Ernst & Young booth manned by a single person who was not talking to anyone. Being curious, I walked up and asked, 'What's the difference between this Ernst & Young booth and the other two (also at the expo)?' The man pointed to the upper level and replied, "That one up there recruits from your top five accounting program. The one over there is for our management consulting practice. I'm here to recruit from a specialized dual degree MBA and MHA (master's in health administration) program."

I explained that I was an undergraduate scheduled to graduate in about six months and that I had once been premed but had decided I liked the business school classes much more than the science curriculum. I also shared I was going to take the GMAT (the exam required for entrance into most MBA programs) and planned to go back to school after gaining a couple of years of work experience.

I left the booth and headed back to my apartment, where I picked up the paper course catalog. Remember, this was 1996. Very limited information appeared on the World Wide Web. I looked up and read the information related to the dual degree MBA—MHA program and immediately thought this could be an interesting path. I reached out to the Department of Health Administration to request some additional information. Upon receiving and reviewing it, I determined that this seemed like a perfect next step.

I took the GMAT and scored pretty well. I applied to the dual degree program at the University of Florida as well as the MBA program at the University of Georgia in Athens. That program would have been much cheaper due to in-state tuition. Unlike my undergraduate applications, these required essays and letters of recommendation. Fortunately, I had taken on several leadership positions during my undergraduate tenure, so I had experiences to write about. I had also worked with some faculty members on various committees and could get their recommendations.

A couple of months later, I learned that both programs had accepted me, so after some deliberations and discussions, I decided to stay in Gainesville, Florida and attend the dual degree program. About 120 people were in the first year of our MBA program and 11 of us were part of the dual degree MBA–MHA class—eight men and three women.

It was an incredible experience, and one where I learned so much from my classmates and my teachers. As part of the MBA program, we were assigned to a group/team and mine, by far, was the most diverse. The group included an Irish Catholic male who was engaged and had earned his undergraduate degree from Notre Dame, an African American female, a homosexual male, a Hispanic male from Miami, and me, a Jewish guy. I was the only one with no work experience, but I knew how the University of Florida worked as well as the city of Gainesville, and I was also pretty good at math. We should have filmed our team meetings—we could have had our own TV show, undoubtedly a hit comedy.

Although most of the MBA students left for summer internships, the MHA program required us to stay and take classes. During that summer, the 11 of us spent a lot of time together, in class and outside. We had two doctors, one who had been practicing for twenty-plus years and one fresh out of medical school. Three gentlemen were active-duty or recently in the military. Our group also had a mix of differences in family types, cultures, religions, sexual orientation, and socioeconomic differences. This was another melting pot of people I learned with and from.

As we entered our second year, several of us were interested in going into consulting. The same gentleman who had manned the Ernst & Young booth two years earlier was still recruiting from our program. Turns out his name is Joe Poats—he was a partner out of the Tampa office. Joe recruited five of us to work at Ernst & Young, including my girlfriend and me, who I had just started dating and somehow eventually convinced to be my wife—for twenty years and counting.

We both thought it would be a two to three-year gig, which would culminate with a move into industry. I worked for six and one-half years in Big 5 consulting. My career started in Ernst & Young's consulting practice, which was bought by Cap Gemini (now Capgemini) and then sold to Accenture. While this was just one job,

I worked for three companies and over a dozen clients, and I made hundreds of connections that I was truly privileged to work with and learn from. My wife stayed one year longer before taking a role at a local hospital. I cannot even imagine how different my life would be if I had not stopped at that Ernst & Young booth and asked a simple question to satisfy my curiosity.

Opportunities come from all sorts of encounters and interactions. Keep a positive attitude and treat every encounter and person as professionally as possible. I like to think of each conversation as a scratch-off lottery ticket. Some are losers, some result in getting more tickets (additional conversations), and one just might be a winner.

You never know when the winner will come, so you always need to be ready by keeping a growth mindset and a sense of curiosity.

I like to think of each conversation as a scratch-off lottery ticket. Some are losers, some result in getting more tickets (additional conversations), and one just might be a winner.

CHAPTER 18

UNTIL NEXT TIME
BE HUMAN, BE HUMBLE,
BE HAPPY

*At the end of the day people won't remember what you
said or did, they will remember how you made them feel.*
—Maya Angelou

Like life itself, Everyday Leadership is a roller coaster. You will have great highs and sometimes tremendous lows. As an Everyday Leader, make it your goal to reduce the number and depths of the lows for everyone so you can spend more time enjoying the high points along the ride. Hopefully the concepts, ideas, and tools that I have shared in this book will allow you to accomplish just that. While Everyday Leadership is simple in theory, practicing it is hard. Obstacles and distractions come your way constantly: the needs and desires of others at home or at work, the requests from friends and people in the community in which you live.

On top of that, you're continually bombarded with offers, alerts, texts, emails, sales pitches, and notifications coming through your electronic devices.

Given all these stressors, you are going to lose focus occasionally, have a bad moment, make the wrong decision, and every now and then regret how you behaved in a given situation. Remember, nobody is perfect. Not even you or me. As you venture out into the jungle of life every day, don't forget that you are on a complicated yet exciting journey—a journey where you will have the opportunity for self-fulfillment as well as the chance to positively impact others' lives. While this book is filled with ideas, stories, and concepts of how to embrace Everyday Leadership, if you take nothing else away, remember this: just Be Human, Be Humble, and Be Happy.

Being human is about recognizing your own feelings and the way others feel too—which, by the way, can be radically different at times!

Take this example. Not too long ago, when my son was 12 years old, he was upset about something. My then two-year-old daughter just walked up and started hugging and petting his leg and then looked up at him and said, "Don't be sad. It's going to be okay." (Yes, Everyday Leadership starts young in our home!) But even though the very best leaders are in fact compassionate problem solvers, that moment just shows that it is natural to be human. We are born to care about each other, to want each other to succeed, and to demonstrate vulnerability by expressing our emotions in a genuine, authentic, and empathetic way.

One of the most authentic speeches I have ever heard was delivered by Jim Valvano. Jim, a college basketball coach, was best known for leading his North Carolina State Wolfpack to a national championship in 1983. Along the way, his team defeated a few heavily favored teams, culminating in a massive upset of the Houston Cougars in the national championship game. After he finished coaching, Valvano remained involved in college basketball and sports as a broadcaster and traveled the country as a motivational speaker. He was diagnosed with cancer in the summer of 1992.

In a February 1993 speech commemorating the ten-year anniversary of his team's 1983 title run, he "stressed the importance of hope, love, and persistence, and included his famous 'Don't give up, don't ever give up' quotation."[33]

Less than two weeks later and approximately two months before his death, he received the inaugural Arthur Ashe Courage and Humanitarian Award at the first ESPN ESPY Awards. During his acceptance speech, he announced the formation of The V Foundation for Cancer Research. Knowing his time was limited, he also shared some wisdom, which included the following:

"To me, there are three things we all should do every day. We should do this every day of our lives. Number one is laugh. You should laugh every day. Number two is think. You should spend some time

---

[33] https://www.reviewob.com/leadership-slam-dunk-lessons-for-ods-from-coach-jimmy-valvano/

in thought. Number three is, you should have your emotions moved to tears, could be happiness or joy. But think about it. If you laugh, you think, and you cry, that's a full day. That's a heck of a day. You do that seven days a week, you're going to have something special."[34]

Computers and artificial intelligence are already beating humans at chess and *Jeopardy* and will get smarter and smarter as they process more and more information. However, no computer can dream, laugh, love, cry, or provide empathy. These human characteristics are what others look for in leaders. Your followers don't need you to be smart; they need you to be genuine and authentic. To quote Tony Robbins, "Don't try to be perfect; just be an excellent example of being human."[35]

A corollary to being human is being humble. I have been humbled over and over, starting with being a captain on my 0–10 varsity football team, to serving as president of my undergraduate fraternity, to leading consulting teams, teaching Junior Achievement to high school students, mentoring an up-and-coming leader, and as an executive transforming the technological infrastructure and overseeing more than 1,500 people and dozens of processes, technologies, and vendor relationships for a $3.5 billion health system. While each of these opportunities were different, they all had one thing

---

34 https://www.si.com/college/ncstate/college/ncstate/basketball/jimmy-v-espy-speech

35 https://www.goodreads.com/quotes/36965-live-life-fully-while-you-re-here-experience-everything-take-care

in common: it was a great privilege and responsibility to have the opportunity to cultivate talent, build teams, share knowledge, and deliver results.

More than any other leap, transitioning from doing to leading was extremely humbling. In every instance, I quickly realized that to be successful it was not about how good I was. Instead, it was about how good of a team I could build and creating a culture that would foster long-term results. On our senior-deprived football team, it was mentoring the juniors and sophomores and setting

---

While Everyday Leadership is simple in theory, practicing it is hard.

---

an example by giving my best even though I was far from the best. While I was president of my fraternity, it was developing financial structure to promote engagement of all classes. With Junior Achievement, it was making time to educate the next generation of leaders on personal finance. Most recently I was given the opportunity to transform, lead, and grow a 500-plus-person team into a 1,500-plus-person team.

It was humbling and rewarding to watch the people on the team I built and supported go out and do their jobs. For example, we hired a communications lead. After I did this, the newsletter I wrote every couple of weeks became a professionally designed and distributed newsletter about 1,000 times better than anything I would have put together. But I also knew I needed to keep connecting with the team, so I started sending out monthly updates that focused on the business, and each became more and more personal over the years, generating connections I never thought were possible. Not being the doer was, and still is, hard for me. I do not like asking for help. But when I do, I have never asked

---

More than any other leap, transitioning from doing to leading was extremely humbling. In every instance, I quickly realized that to be successful it was not about how good I was. Instead, it was about how good of a team I could build and creating a culture that would foster long-term results.

---

anyone to do anything I would not do myself. I just keep reminding myself that if I am spending my day entering formulas in a spreadsheet, which I love to do, then I am doing someone else's job and mine is not getting done.

While all of those experiences were humbling and rewarding, nothing gives you humility like being a parent. You want the best for your kids, and you try to give them opportunities to succeed. Even so, they must learn through their own experiences. Whether you are at home, in the office, or anywhere else for that matter, you can't learn lessons for other people. Being humble requires you to know your limits and boundaries. It is important to let children have learning experiences on the little things while you teach them the principles and foundational values that you hope they will apply to the big things. It will try your patience like nothing else, but just as you do at work, you must constantly try to set the best example. These little people watch everything you do. Humbling indeed.

Nothing challenges you to step up your leadership game like parenting.

As a parent I now have an enhanced appreciation for my parents, grandparents, and the many generations of family members and friends who sacrificed things I will never know or understand to make this country, our community, and my life better. Through efforts and desire to fight, literally and figuratively, even sometimes surrendering their own hopes, dreams, and desires, they have provided me and future generations the foundation to live a better life. That is truly humbling. I try to respect those sacrifices by focusing on the impact I have made on people and organizations through some combination of luck, curiosity, hard work, and resourcefulness to, if nothing else, keep my family name off the front page of the paper.

While I hope to never experience a world war or the pains and adversity of those who came before me, I do choose to carry the lessons of my elders and the knowledge of the atrocities and sins against humanity that have shaped the world we live in today. In doing so, I hope to make better choices so I "solve more problems than I cause" and make the world, or at least my corner of it, a better place as a parent, coach, executive, and Everyday Leader during my time on this planet.

Regardless of your age, it is a gift to be able to make a difference. But you must take action, by actively seeking out ways to make life better for those around you. We are only here for a short time, and those who refuse to use their gifts to benefit others are living a life that's less than extraordinary.

I often hear people say that their days are long. Usually it's something along the lines of, "oh what a looonng day."

Every once in a while, it comes from a place of joy and happiness, like the day my son and I spent sixteen hours at Walt Disney World or the times I drove for an hour twice on a Friday, twice on a Saturday, and again twice on a Sunday so he could play in a tennis tournament. Those were long days, but joyful ones!

But most often when people say it, it comes from a place of dread in dealing with their day-to-day work, or unhappiness. While the days may be long, the years are short. If you live in a state of constant unhappiness, it will wear down your mind, body, and soul. It will take a physical and emotional toll on those around you as well. Consider that great leadership involves managing yourself and your mindset too. If you're not happy, it's as contagious as if you are, so make it a point to attend to your emotional wellness.

People do not want to be around (much less follow) unhappy people. Simple as that. Organizations take on the characteristics of their leaders. The leaders set the tone and culture for their organizations. You see this in sports teams, businesses, and families. In sports, it could be the owner or the head coach or manager. In business, it is usually the CEO or leader of a division. At school, it is the principal or the teacher, and at home it is the parents. No matter the organization, someone at the top is setting the tone for how the players, team members, and students, or kids operate and play. Is everyone edgy and quick to blame others for their mistakes? Look to the leader of the organization, and you'll see someone demonstrating that behavior every day.

When I work with leaders on improvement, it often becomes clear that they don't even recognize their toxic or ineffective behaviors. But those around them sure do!

The bottom line is that you need to be happy to be an effective Everyday Leader in the boardroom, playroom, ballroom, classroom, emergency room, locker room, and virtual team room. Be happy for yourself, your family, and your team at work. A positive attitude, a glass half-full mentality, and happiness will make those long days pass by faster and the years more enjoyable as you live to love and experience all of life and the wonders our planet has to offer and the opportunities for fulfillment that Everyday Leadership can provide.

So if you take nothing else from this book, Be Human, Be Humble, and Be Happy.

PERSPECTIVES   WHEREFROM   GRANDPARENT   TEAM
UNDERSTAND   BUSINESS EXECUTIVE   LOCKER ROOM
TOGETHER   HELP OTHERS   HOBBIES   EMPOWERING
SOLVE MORE PROBLEMS THAN YOU CAUSE   IMPROVE
COMMUNICATION   CANDID   THINK DIFFERENTLY
TOWARDS THE FUTURE   BELIEVE   POSITIVE INTENT
INCREASE YOUR KNOWLEDGE   BEST   SELF-AWARE
INTEGRITY   CLARITY
RELATIONSHIPS   GROWTH MINDSET   GENUINE   HUMBLE
SEPARATE FACTS FROM FAIRY TALES   EXPECTATIONS
TEACHER   FAILURE IS NECESSARY   CONNECT THE DOTS

SPECIAL THANKS TO...

My wife Hilary, who is my biggest supporter but also a realist who tells me what I need to hear and keeps me grounded. I am fortunate our paths crossed and grateful for everything you do every day for us and our kids. Just like everything else in our lives, I could not have done this without you. I love you and you are the best!

My kids Harris and Sara, who have taught me more about myself in the last 13 and 4 years respectively than I learned in my first 35 years and 44 without you. Hopefully this book will keep you from making the same stupid mistakes as your dad.

Mom and Dad for instilling a core set of values, teaching me what is really important, providing an environment where I could learn, grow, and try new things, and for always being there while allowing me to make my own choices.

Justin Spizman, Book Architect extraordinaire and my coach for this project. Your guidance, questions, challenges, encouragement, direction, and experience made this pipe dream a reality.

SPECIAL THANKS TO...

Norma Zeringue, Joshua **Silver**, Bruce Pulver, and Jyoti Rajagopal for taking time to read early versions of the manuscript and providing me the honest feedback required to make the book better.

Paul Aldo, Jeanette Matern, and Rob Williams for coaching, perspectives, wisdom, and encouragement that comes from decades of working with individuals and teams across different industries.

Michael Brody-Waite, Shay Eskew, Molly Fletcher, Randy Gravitt, Mark Hurst, Colby Johnson, Jim Knight, Sheila Margolis, Quinn (Erin) O'Briant, Bruce Pulver, Jason Ogden, Nido Qubein, Michael Rovinsky, Saleema Vellani, Jonathan Wiik, and Bethany Williams for sharing your journey and lessons learned as you turned ideas into books, blogs, speaking engagements, and/or businesses.

Tammy Kling and the team from OnFire Books, who provided "interior decorating" to make sure the details of the book resonated with you—the reader—and for helping me navigate the jungle that is book marketing and promotion.

Shane Crabtree at Clovercroft Publishing who should have gotten hazard pay for the time he spent facilitating the process of transforming my manuscript into the book you are reading.

Lauren Unell (my sister-in-law) for taking head-shots for the book and cover. To learn more about her passion check out some of her photos on Instagram @ Paleskyphotos.

Debbie Manning Sheppard for going through iteration after iteration to incorporate my tweaks for the cover.

Tina Fleming for creating the digital awareness needed to promote a book in the twenty first century.

Angie Kiesling and Becky Taylor for providing professional editing to a first-time author with an undergraduate degree in Statistics. Your ability to fix grammar, improve readability, and ensure the point is made without losing my voice is a tremendous skill.

Countless family members (from my brother Robert to extended cousins), classmates (from grade school through grad school), colleagues (from summer jobs, consulting, and industry), and friends (from birth to those I've met more recently) for providing your personal and professional support all while accepting my quirks and idiosyncrasies.

PERSPECTIVES   WHEREFROM   GRANDPARENT   TEAM
UNDERSTAND   BUSINESS EXECUTIVE   LOCKER ROOM
TOGETHER   HELP OTHERS   HOBBIES   EMPOWERING
SOLVE MORE PROBLEMS THAN YOU CAUSE   IMPROVE
COMMUNICATION   CANDID   THINK DIFFERENTLY
TOWARDS THE FUTURE   BELIEVE   POSITIVE INTENT
INCREASE YOUR KNOWLEDGE   BEST   SELF-AWARE
INTEGRITY   CLARITY
RELATIONSHIPS   GROWTH MINDSET   GENUINE   HUMBLE
SEPARATE FACTS FROM FAIRY TALES   EXPECTATIONS
TEACHER   FAILURE IS NECESSARY   CONNECT THE DOTS

ABOUT THE AUTHOR

Brian Unell describes himself as a recovering Big 5 consultant and health care administrator, while others portray Brian as a transformational health care executive who has a passion for cultivating talent and driving change to enable sustainable results. Brian is recognized as a visionary and collaborative team builder and servant leader who views issues / opportunities from all perspectives, turns data into information, the complex into simple, and chaos into focus. Brian's professional experiences include leading transformational consulting projects, a $180M technology implementation, and a team of 1,500 people. His personal experiences include serving on non-profit boards, mentoring others, and co-leading a team of four at home with his wife Hilary. Both provide the foundation for his stories, concepts, and ideas that make up this first book in what he hopes to be a series on leadership. Brian holds three degrees from the University of Florida: BS-Statistics, Master of Business Administration, & Master of Health Administration. Brian currently resides in his hometown of Atlanta, Georgia with Hilary and their children Harris and Sara where he avidly cheers on the Gators and local professional sports teams.

Connect with Brian

Website: www.brianunell.com

LinkedIn: www.linkedin.com/in/brianunell

Twitter: @BrianUnell

Email: brian@brianunell.com